Lisbon

Fodor's 90
Lisbon

Reprinted from *Fodor's Portugal '90*

FODOR'S TRAVEL PUBLICATIONS, INC.
New York & London

Fodor's Lisbon

Editor: Richard Moore
Assistant Editors: Caz Philcox, Barbara Vesey
Area Editors: Susan Lowndes, Lesley McSeveney
Editorial Contributors: Robert Brown, Mark Lewes
Cartography: R.P. Gossop, Swanston Graphics
Drawings: Lorraine Calaora
Cover Photograph: Tony Arruza/Bruce Coleman Inc.

Cover Design: Vignelli Associates

CONTENTS

FOREWORD

Of all European capitals, Lisbon is perhaps the one least trampled by the March of Time. Indeed, under the long dictatorship of Dr. Salazar, time stood still for the whole of Portugal, and it is only since the revolution of 1974 that modern life has started to make any headway there. The process of bringing the country into the 20th century will now speed up as the conditions of entry into the European Economic Community start to take hold.

Lisbon may be a comparatively poor city as European capitals go, but it still preserves the slightly mysterious air of the capital of a nation separated from the rest of the continent by its history and its blood; of a nation more used to looking overseas than eastward to its more powerful neighbors; of a nation that, even in today's speeding world, preserves folkways that can be colorful and very strange.

To see Lisbon from the deck of the Tagus ferry, with the castle, the cathedral and the old houses on their eastern hill, and the exciting new highrise blocks piercing the skyline to westward, is to see a panorama of the new Portugal. To plunge into the attractive squares, the climbing alleys, and Baroque churches, is to revisit a world that is largely lost to the rest of Europe.

*

While every care has been taken to assure the accuracy of the information in this guide, the passage of time will always bring change, and consequently the publisher cannot accpet responsibility for errors that may occur.

All prices and opening times quoted in this guide are based on information available to us at press time. Hours and admission fees may change, however, and the prudent traveler will avoid inconvenience by calling ahead.

Fodor's wants to hear about your travel experiences, both pleasant and unpleasant. When a hotel or restaurant fails to live up to its billing, let us know and we will investigate the complaint and revise our entries where the facts warrant it.

Send your letters to the editors of Fodor's Travel Publications, 201 E. 50th Street, New York, NY 10022.

FACTS AT YOUR FINGERTIPS

Planning Your Trip

NATIONAL TOURIST OFFICE. One of the very best sources of information, brochures and suggestions for helping you plan your trip in general, is the Portuguese National Tourist Office. Casa de Portugal information offices are located in—**New York:** 590 Fifth Avenue, New York, N.Y. 10036 (tel. 212–354–4403). **Toronto:** 2180 Yonge St., Toronto, Ontario M4S 2B9 (tel. 416–487–3300). **London:** New Bond Street House, 1–5 New Bond St., London W1Y 0NP (tel. 493 3873).

WHEN TO GO. Portugal has a temperate climate, and the tourist season begins in spring and lasts through the fall. Average afternoon temperatures in Lisbon, in Fahrenheit and Centigrade:

	Jan.	Feb.	Mar.	Apr.	May	June	July	Aug.	Sept.	Oct.	Nov.	Dec.
F°	56	58	61	64	69	75	79	80	76	69	62	57
C°	13	14	16	18	21	24	26	27	24	21	17	14

National Holidays. January 1 (New Year's Day), February 7 (Carnival), April 13 (Good Friday), April 25 (Anniversary of Revolution), May 1 (Labor Day), May 25 (Corpus Christi), June 10 (National Day), August 15 (Assumption), October 5 (Republic Day), November 1 (All Saints Day), December 1 (Restoration of Independence), December 8 (Immaculate Conception), and Christmas Day.

WHAT TO TAKE. The first principle is to travel light. Regulations concerning baggage on transatlantic flights vary slightly from airline to airline, so check with yours before you go. In general, however, these are the rules: passengers are allowed to check two pieces of luggage, and carry on one. Checked luggage is restricted by weight (the maximum is usually 32 kg., 70 lbs.) and by total dimensions (that is, the total of the piece's height, width, and depth) which should be no more than 1.57 meters (62 inches) for one piece and 1.47 meters (58 inches) for the second. Carry-on luggage must be small enough to fit under a seat, or in the compartment above the seats. These rules all apply to economy-class passengers; first-class travelers are often allowed a few extra inches' total dimension. If your bags are larger, heavier, or if you want to bring more than three pieces, you will have to pay an excess baggage charge. Please note that these rules apply to transatlantic flights only. If, after breaking your journey, you fly on to the Continent or beyond, the rules may well be different, and based on weight. Again, check before you go.

Most bus lines as well as a few of the crack international trains place limits on the weight (usually 25 kg., 55 lbs.) or bulk of your luggage.

Resist the temptation to take more than two suitcases per person in your party, or to select luggage larger than you can carry yourself. Porters are increasingly scarce these days and you will face delays every time you change trains, or hotels, go through customs, or otherwise try to move about with the freedom that today's travelers enjoy.

Motorists should limit luggage to what can be locked in the trunk or boot of the car when daytime stops are made. Theft from cars in Portugal is not as serious a problem as in neighboring Spain, but it is not unknown. At night, everything should be removed to your hotel room.

TAKING MONEY ABROAD. Traveler's checks are still the standard and best way to safeguard your travel funds and you still usually get a better exchange rate in Portugal for traveler's checks than for cash. In the U.S., many of the larger banks issue their own traveler's checks—just about as universally recognized as those of *American Express, Cook's* and *Barclay's.* In most instances there is a 1% charge for the checks; there is no fee for Barclay's checks. Some banks also issue them free if you are a regular customer. The best-known British checks are *Cook's* and those of *Barclay's, Lloyd's,* the *Midland Bank* and the *Nat West,* and of course *American Express.* It is also always a good idea to have some local currency upon arrival. Some banks will provide this service; alternately, contact *Deak International,* 630 Fifth Ave., New York, N.Y. 10011 (212–635–0515), call for additional branches.

Britons holding a *Eurocheque Card* and check book can cash checks for up to £100 a day at banks participating in the scheme and can write checks in hotels, restaurants and shops again for up to £100. Look for the distinctive blue and red symbol in the window. To obtain a card and check book, apply at your bank.

Credit Cards. The major credit cards—*American Express, Diner's Club, MasterCard* (incorporating *Access* and *EuroCard*) and *Visa*—are generally but by no means universally accepted in most larger hotels, restaurants and shops. We give details on which of these cards is accepted by the hotels and restaurants we carry in our *Practical Information* listings. We have indicated them with the abbreviations AE, DC, MC, V. But always be sure to check before reserving your room or ordering a meal that your particular piece, or pieces, of plastic is accepted.

CURRENCY. As exchange rates are currently so volatile, we suggest you check on them while planning your trip, and keep a very close eye on what the escudo is up to while you are traveling. There are 100 centavos to an escudo.

Note: The symbol for the escudo is a $ sign, written between the escudo and the centavo units—thus 100$00. At presstime (mid-1989) the exchange rate was about 160$00 escudos to the U.S. dollar and 260$00 escudos to the pound sterling.

We would like to suggest that you take with you some small denomination of Portuguese money to help with porters, taxis and such on arrival. It is not always possible, or convenient, to change travelers' checks immediately.

There are notes of 5,000, 1,000, 500, and 100 escudos, and coins of 100, 50, 25, 10, 5, 2½ and 1 escudos and of 50 centavos. Newly minted 1-, 5-, and 10-escudo yellow-colored coins can be confused for older coins still in circulation, so make sure you know exactly what you're spending.

TRAVEL DOCUMENTS. Getting a passport should have priority in your plans. **U.S. residents** must apply in person and several months in advance of their expected departure date to the U.S. Passport Agency in Boston, Chicago, Honolulu, Los Angeles, Miami, New Orleans, New York, Philadelphia, San Francisco, Seattle, Stamford, Conn., Washington D.C., or to their local county courthouse. In some areas selected post offices are also equipped to handle passport applications. If you still have your latest previous passport issued within the past 12 years, you may use this to apply by mail. Otherwise, take with you your birth certificate or certified copy, 2 identical photographs 2″ square, on non-glossy paper, color or black and white, taken within the past six months, proof of identity such as a driving license, and $35, plus a $7 processing fee (you can apply by mail and save the processing fee). For those under 18 years old, passports cost $20, plus the $7 fee. Passports are valid for 10 years, 5 years for those under 18, and are nonrenewable. If you expect to travel widely you may ask for a 48- or 96-page passport instead of the usual 24-page one. There is no extra charge. If your passport gets lost or stolen, immediately notify the nearest American Consulate or the Passport Office, Department of State, Washington, D.C. 20524. Record your passport's number and its place and date of issue in a separate, secure place.

If you are not an American citizen, but are leaving from the U.S., you must have a Treasury Sailing Permit, Form 1040C or short Form 2063, certifying that all Federal taxes have been paid—apply to your District Director of Internal Revenue; you will also have to present a blue or green alien registration card, passport, travel tickets, most recently filed Form 1040, W2 forms for the last full year, current payroll stubs or letter—and maybe more, so check.

To return to the U.S., you need a re-entry permit if you intend to stay away longer than one year. Apply for it at least 6 weeks before departure in person at the nearest office of the Immigration and Naturalization Service, or by mail to the Immigration and Naturalization Service, Washington, D.C.

Canadian citizens in Canada should apply in person to regional passport offices or write to the Bureau of Passports, External Affairs, Ottawa, Ontario K1A 0G3 (tel. 819–994–3500). A fee of $25, evidence of citizenship, a guarantor, and 2 photographs are required. Canadian citizens living in the U.S. need special forms available at their nearest Canadian Consulate.

British citizens: Apply through your travel agency. The application should be sent to the passport office for your area, as indicated on the guidance form, or taken personally to the nearest main post office. Apply at least 5 weeks before the passport is required. The regional passport offices are located in London, Liverpool, Peterborough, Glasgow, Newport (Gwent), and Belfast. The application must be countersigned by your bank manager or by a solicitor, barrister, doctor, clergyman, or Justice of the Peace who knows you personally. You will need 2 full-face photos. The current fee is £15. (A cost rise is expected.) Valid for 10 years.

British Visitor's Passport: This simplified form of passport has advantages for the once-in-a-while tourist to Portugal and most other European countries. Valid for 1 year and not renewable, it costs £7.50. Application must be made in person at a main post office; proof of identity and 2 passport photographs are required—no other formalities.

Incidentally, when you have your passport photos made, order about 6 extra prints. These come in handy for international driver's licenses and similar purposes that are difficult to foresee.

Visas. Neither American nor British citizens need a visa to visit mainland Portugal, Madeira or the Azores for stays up to 60 days. For longer stays, apply to the police for an extension, when the original 60 days is about to end.

Visitors believed to be entering the country without sufficient funds may be asked to show that they have a minimum of 500$00 per day for the length of their stay in the country. This regulation is designed to discourage hitchhikers from begging or dealing in drugs to pay their way. This became quite a problem, in the Algarve principally, and later spread elsewhere.

Health Certificates. Not required for entry into Portugal. Neither the U.S. nor Canada requires a certificate of vaccination prior to re-entry. Because of frequent changes in law, we suggest you check up before you leave.

HEALTH AND INSURANCE. The first thing to do when considering your insurance needs for an upcoming trip is to look at the coverage you've already got. Most major insurers (*Blue Cross/Blue Shield, Metropolitan Life,* etc.) treat sickness, injury and death abroad no differently than they treat them at home. If, however, you find that your existing insurance comes up short in some significant way (most do not cover the costs of emergency evacuation, for example); or if you would like help finding medical aid abroad, as well as paying for it; or if you would like coverage against those most vexing travel bedevilments, baggage loss and cancellation of your trip, then you may want to consider buying travel insurance.

Your travel agent is a good source of information on travel insurance. She or he should have an idea of the insurance demands of different destinations; moreover, several of the traveler's insurance companies retail exclusively through travel agents. The *American Society of Travel Agents* endorses the *Travel Guard* plan, issued by *The Insurance Company of North America.* Travel Guard offers an insurance package that includes coverage for sickness, injury or death, lost baggage, and interruption or cancellation of your trip. Lost baggage coverage will also cover unauthorized use of your credit cards, while trip cancellation or interruption coverage will reimburse you for additional costs incurred due to a sudden halt (or failed start) to your trip. The Travel Guard Gold program has three plans: advance purchase, for trips up to 30 days ($19); super advance purchase, for trips up to 45 days ($39); and comprehensive, for trips up to 180 days (8% of the cost of travel). Optional features with the Travel Guard Gold program include cancellation and supplemental CDW (collision damage waiver) coverage. For more information, talk to your travel agent, or *Travel Guard,* 1100 Center Point Dr., Stevens Point, WI 54481 (tel. 800–782–5151).

The *Travelers Companies* has a *Travel Insurance Pak,* also sold through travel agents. It is broken down into three parts: Travel Accident Coverage (sickness, injury, or death), Baggage Loss, and Trip Cancellation. Any one of the three parts can be bought separately. Cost of the accident and baggage loss coverage depends on the amount of coverage desired and the length of your stay. Two weeks of accident coverage can cost approximately $20; baggage coverage for the same length of time costs $30. The cost of trip cancellation coverage depends on the cost of your travel; the rate is $5.50 per $100 of travel expenses. Again, your travel agent should have full details, or you can get in touch with the *Travelers Companies,* Ticket and Travel, One Tower Square, Hartford, CT 06183 (tel. 800–243–3174).

If an accident occurs, paying for medical care may be a less urgent problem than finding it. Several companies offer emergency medical assistance along with insurance. *Access America* offers travel insurance and the assistance of a 24-hour hotline in Washington, D.C. that can direct distressed travelers to a nearby source of aid. They maintain contact with a worldwide network of doctors, hospitals and pharmacies, offer medical evacuation services (a particular problem if you're hurt in an out-of-the-way spot), on-site cash provision services (if it's needed to pay for medical care), legal assistance, and help with lost documents and ticket replacement. Access America offers its services through travel agents and Triple A. Cost ranges from $5–$10 per day. For more information, *Access America,* 600 Third Avenue, Box 807, New York, N.Y. 10163 (tel. 800–851–2800).

Other organizations that offer similar assistance are:

Carefree Travel Insurance, c/o ARM Coverage, Inc., 120 Mineola Blvd., Box 310, Mineola, N.Y. 11501 (tel. 516–293–0220), offers medical evacuation arranged through Europe Assistance of Paris.

International SOS Assistance, Inc., Box 11568, Philadelphia, PA. 19116 (tel. 1–800–523–8930) charges from $15 a person for seven days to $195 for a year.

IAMAT (International Association for Medical Assistance to Travelers), 417 Center St., Lewiston, N.Y. 14092 (tel. 716–754–4883); 40 Regal Rd., Guelph, Ontario N1K 1B5 (tel. 519–836–0102).

Travel Assistance International, the American arm of Europ Assistance, offers a comprehensive program offering immediate, on-the-spot medical, personal and financial help. Trip protection ranges from $40 for an individual for up to eight days to $600 for an entire family for a year. For full details, contact your travel agent or insurance broker, or write Europ Assistance Worldwide Services Inc., 1133 15th St. NW, Suite 400, Washington, DC 20005 (800–821–2828). In the U.K., contact *Europ Assistance Ltd.,* 252 High St., Croydon, Surrey (tel. 01–680 1234).

The Association of British Insurers, Aldermary House, 10–15 Queen St., London EC4N 1TT (tel. 01–248 4477), will give comprehensive advice on all aspects of vacation travel insurance from the U.K.

Medical Treatment. In Portugal, there is no free medical treatment for visitors unless their countries of origin have reciprocal health agreements, as between the U.K. and Portugal. Nationals and residents benefit according to their employment. There is a British Hospital at Rua Saraiva de Carvalho 49, Lisbon (tel. 602020 during the day, 603785 at night), for both in- and outpatients, with English-speaking doctors and nurses.

HINTS FOR DISABLED TRAVELERS. Tours specially designed for the disabled generally parallel those of the non-disabled traveler, but at a more leisurely pace. For a complete list of tour operators who arrange such travel write to the *Society for the Advancement of Travel for the Handicapped,* 26 Court St., Brooklyn, N.Y. 11242. *Moss Rehabilitation Hospital,* 12th St. and Tabor Rd., Philadelphia, PA 19141, answers inquiries regarding specific cities and countries as well as providing toll-free telephone numbers for airlines with special lines for the hearing impaired and, again, listings of selected tour operators. The fee is $5 per destination. Allow one month for delivery.

The *International Air Transport Association* (IATA) publishes a free pamphlet, *Incapacitated Passengers' Air Travel Guide,* explaining the various arrangements to be made and how to make them. Write IATA, 2000 Peel St., Montreal, Quebec H3A 2R4.

In the U.K., contact *Mobility International,* 228 Borough High St., London SE1 1JX; the *Royal Society for Mentally Handicapped Adults and Children* (MENCAP), 117 Golden Lane, London EC1 ORT; the *Across Trust,* Crown House, Morden, Surrey (they have an amazing series of "Jumbulances," huge articulated ambulances, staffed by volunteer doctors and nurses, that can whisk even the most seriously disabled across Europe in comfort and safety). But the main source in Britain for all advice on handicapped travel is the *Royal Association for Disability and Rehabilitation* (RADAR), 25 Mortimer St., London W1N 8AB.

Getting To Lisbon

FROM NORTH AMERICA BY AIR. Two airlines fly from the U.S. to Portugal: *TAP Air Portugal* and *TWA.* TAP flies daily out of New York, and twice weekly out of Boston and Los Angeles. TWA flies daily out of New York only. From Canada, *Air Canada* flies thrice weekly services from Toronto and Montreal to Lisbon; *TAP Air Portugal* has frequent services both from Montreal and Toronto.

In the past few years, airlines have beefed up security on international flights considerably. That translates into more time getting on and off a plane. Be sure to leave yourself plenty of time at the airport arriving and departing.

Air Canada, Place Air Canada, 500 Dorchester Blvd., Montreal, Quebec H2Z 1X5 (tel. 514–393–3333).

TAP Air Portugal, 1140 Ave. of the Americas, New York, N.Y. 10036 (tel. 800–221–7370).

TWA, 100 S. Bedford Rd., Mt. Kisco, NY 10549 (tel. 212–290–2141).

Fares generally come in four categories, which are, in descending order of expense, First Class, Business, Economy, and APEX. The first three are usually sold without restrictions; they can be bought, used, cancelled or changed at any time. They are distinguished from one another by where they seat you on the plane, and what sort of freebies are attached to your travel (e.g. champagne, etc.). They are also all quite expensive compared to the fourth, APEX.

APEX tickets are always round-trip, seat the passenger in the economy section, and are subject to several conditions. They must be bought well in advance of the flight (7–21 days); they limit the times and days one can fly, and they restrict the length of your travel; they usually require a minimum stay of seven days, and a maximum of three months. They are also quite inexpensive compared to the other tickets. In mid-1989, round-trip New York-Lisbon fares were: First Class, $3,726; Business Class (TAP calls it Navigator Class), $2,076; Economy, $1,362; APEX, from $685. Note that TAP Air Portugal does not offer First Class service.

For even greater savings, tickets on charter flights are sometimes available. Check with your travel agent. There are also a number of ticket brokers who sell seats on flights ordered by tour operators that are not quite completely booked. Note that these tickets are usually available only on very short notice. Among the brokers are: *Stand-buys Ltd.,* 831 Greencrest Dr., Westerville, OH 43081 (tel. 800–255–1488); *Moments Notice,* 40 E. 49th St., New York, N.Y. 10017 (tel. 212–486–0503); *Discount Travel Int'l,* 114 Forest Ave., Narberth, PA 19072 (tel. 215–668–2182); and *Worldwide Discount Travel Club,* 1674 Meridian Ave., Miami Beach, FL 33139 (tel. 305–534–2082).

FROM THE U.K. BY AIR. During the summer there is one flight daily from London Heathrow to Lisbon by *British Airways* (tel. 01–897–4000) and one flight daily from Heathrow by *TAP Air Portugal* (two flights daily on Thursdays, Saturdays, and Sundays). TAP's number is 01–828–0262. The flying time is two hours 35 minutes. There is also a BA flight every day (except Tuesday and Saturday) from London Gatwick airport. Flying BA to Lisbon a roundtrip in Club Class costs around £396, £150–£209 for a Super-Pex return. Book and pay at any time before departure.

Staying In Lisbon

CUSTOMS. You are allowed to bring into Portugal such personal possessions as typewriters, cameras, movie cameras, tape-recorders, portable radios, tents and camping equipment, sports equipment like fishing gear, hunting rifles with 50 cartridges, a kayak 5.5 meters (18 ft.) long (maximum), tennis racquets, etc. You are also entitled to bring in 200 cigarettes or $\frac{1}{2}$ lb of tobacco, a bottle of wine, a quart of liquor, an ordinary amount of perfume.

HOTELS. Hotels are graded into categories based on quality and prices: 5-star (deluxe), 4-, 3-, 2-, and 1-star. These roughly equate to our categories of Deluxe (L), Expensive (E), Moderate (M), and Inexpensive (I). Hotel prices are no longer state controlled.

Daily Bed and Breakfast Room Rates

Approximate High-Season Rates for Two in Escudos

Deluxe (L)	25,000–35,000
Expensive (E)	17,000–25,000
Moderate (M)	10,000–17,000

Inexpensive (I) under 10,000
Service and tourist taxes are usually included.

Hotels in the (L), (E) and (M) price categories will have all rooms with bath, while those in the (I) category will have most rooms with bath. Pensions run from 3,500$00–5,000$00 for a room with bath, 2,500$00–4,000$00 without. The Portuguese word is *pensão*.

If breakfast is not included in the hotel rate, this will cost from 300$00. Lunch or dinner at a good restaurant will run from around 3,000$00 each, depending on the wines chosen. Service and taxes are usually included in the bill but a 5% to 10% tip should be given. All restaurants have their price lists displayed outside. Inexpensive restaurants don't take reservations for tables.

Note: These are the rates as we go to press in mid-1989. In the present financial situation they may well have risen by the beginning of 1990, so check in advance.

If you haven't reserved any hotel accommodation in advance you can make enquiries at the Information Service of the Direcção-Geral do Turismo, Palacio Foz, Praça dos Restauradores or Ave. António Augusto Aguiar 86.

RESTAURANTS. Although we grade our restaurant listings Expensive (E), Moderate (M), and Inexpensive (I), as usual, there are very few Expensive restaurants outside the major towns or main tourist areas. In comparison with the States or Britain, eating is very reasonable in Portugal, reasonable and hearty. Portions are generally large, except in really top-class places, and you'll find yourself having only one big meal a day without any problem at all. Our grading is aligned to the following price ranges—(E) 4,000$00–6,000$00, (M) 2,000$00–4,000$00, (I) under 2,000$00 per person, without alcohol.

TIPPING. Hotel service charges cover everything. But give 100$00 per bag to whoever brings the luggage up. A nightclub waiter expects 10% in addition to the service charge. Station porters expect 100$00 per bag, hatcheck girls, theater ushers, the same; 50$00 escudos for bootblacks. Taxi drivers get 5 to 10%. Gas station attendants 25$00 to 50$00. In barbershops, men give 50$00, while in average beauty salons women tip 100$00, in more elaborate ones 200$00.

Although a service charge is usually included in the check at restaurants, cafés, etc., a small tip is always welcome (about 5% in a moderate restaurant). Especially wise if you intend to return.

CLOSING TIMES. Banks are open 8:30–11:45 and 1–2:45 Mondays to Fridays, but many private banks now open through lunch. There is also an automatic currency machine at Praça dos Restauradores. Shops usually open from 9 to 1 and 3 to 7 Mondays to Fridays, 9 to 1 Saturdays. Shopping centers and supermarkets tend to stay open till midnight and also on Sundays. Museums in Lisbon and most other places are closed Mondays and holidays, open 10–5 other days, including Sundays, but usually close for lunch. Palaces in Lisbon close on Tuesdays.

MAIL. Postal rates, both domestic and foreign, increase from time to time, especially in the present uncertain economic climate. Sub-post offices open 9–12:30, 2:30–6 on weekdays. Some main offices stay open at lunchtime.

Stamp collectors may find treasures, or simply enjoy a leisurely visit to the *Clube Filatélico de Portugal*, 70 Ave. Almirante Reis, 5th floor, or to *Numifilarte*, Calçada do Carmo 25, *Molder*, Rua 1 Dezembro 101, 3rd floor, *Eládio de Santos*, 27 Rua Bernado Lima, all in Lisbon. Look under *Filatelia* in the Yellow Pages for further addresses.

ELECTRICITY. Voltage 220 AC. In a few remote areas, 110 volts.

DRINKING WATER. Water is usually safe to drink, but use one or other of the excellent mineral waters if you want to play safe. *Luso* is still *(sem gas)*, *Agua de Castelo* fizzy *(com gas)*. Pasteurized milk is available in most towns.

HINTS FOR BUSINESSPEOPLE. Normal office hours in Portugal are from 9 to 5 or 5:30 with a 2-hour break for lunch from 1 to 3, but don't expect to see the managing director before 10. Coffee is often offered to clients, but no one minds if it is refused. Smoking is declining, but again no one minds if you smoke.

Shake hands wherever you go, turn as you get out of sight to bow or wave to your host who will be standing at the door until you are out of his vision and do the same to him if he comes to your office or hotel. Men should normally be addressed as Senhor Doutor if they are lawyers or medical men, as Senhor Engenheiro if they are engineers and Senhor Arquitecto if they are architects, women as Senhora Doutora, Senhora Engenheira or Senhora Arquitecta. Indeed, every university graduate is called Senhor Doutor or Senhora Doutora, so it does no harm and is flattering to do so if in doubt.

The *Hospedeiras de Portugal*, Rua Borges Carneiro 63–3D, Lisbon 1200, tel. 01 604353, can provide interpreters, translators and secretarial assistance.

It is now considerably cheaper and more satisfactory to telephone abroad than to send cables. All good hotels have telexes, and many fax machines.

Leaving Lisbon

CUSTOMS. Americans who are out of the United States at least 48 hours and have claimed no exemption during the previous 30 days are entitled to bring in duty-free up to $400 worth of articles for bona fide gifts or for their own personal use. The next $1,000 worth of material will be assessed a flat 10% duty. After that, the rate varies, depending on the value of the merchandise. The value of each item is determined by the price actually paid (so save your receipts). Every member of a family is entitled to this same exemption, regardless of age, and the allowance can be pooled.

Not more than 100 cigars and 200 cigarettes may be imported duty-free per person, nor more than a quart of wine or liquor (none at all if your passport indicates you are from a "dry" state, or if you are under 21 years of age). Only one bottle of perfume that is trademarked in the United States may be brought in, plus a reasonable quantity of other brands.

Gifts which cost less than $50 may be mailed to friends or relatives at home, but not more than one per day (of receipt) to any one addressee. Mark the package "Unsolicited Gift/Value less than $50." These gifts must not include perfumes costing more than $5, tobacco or liquor. However, they do not count as part of your $400 exemption.

Do not bring home foreign meats, fruits, plants, soil, or other agricultural items when you return to the United States. To do so will delay you at the port of entry. It is illegal to bring in foreign agricultural items without permission, because they can spread destructive plant or animal pests and diseases. For more information, read the pamphlet *Customs Hints* or write to Animal and Plant Health Inspection Service, Department of Agriculture, Federal Center Bldg., Hyattsville, Maryland 20782, and ask for Program Aid No. 1083, entitled *Travelers' Tips on Bringing Food, Plant and Animal Produce into the United States.*

If your purchases exceed your exemption, list the items that are subject to the highest rates of duty under your exemption and pay duty on the items with the lowest rates. Any articles you fail to declare cannot later be claimed under your exemption. To facilitate the actual customs examination it's convenient to pack all your purchases in one suitcase.

Purchases intended for your duty-free quota can no longer be sent home separately—they must accompany your personal baggage.

Canadian citizens. In addition to personal effects, the following articles may be brought in duty-free: a maximum of 50 cigars, 200 cigarettes, 2 pounds of tobacco, and 40 ounces of liquor, provided these are declared in writing to customs on arrival and accompany the traveler in hand or checked-through baggage. These are included in the basic exemption of $300 a year. Personal gifts should be mailed as "Unsolicited Gift—Value Under $40."

British citizens. There is now a two-tier allowance for duty-free goods brought into the U.K. due to Britain's Common Market membership. **Note:** The Customs and Excise Board warn that it is not advisable to mix the two allowances.

If you return from an E.E.C. country (Belgium, Denmark, France, W. Germany, Greece, Holland, Italy, Luxembourg, Ireland, Britain—and, since 1986, Portugal and Spain) and goods were bought in one of those countries, duty-free allowances are: 300 cigarettes (or 150 cigarillos, or 75 cigars, or 400g tobacco); 1.5 liters of alcoholic drinks over 22% vol. (38.8DG proof) *or* 3 liters of alcoholic drinks not over 22% vol. *or* fortified *or* sparkling *or* still wine, plus 5 liters of still table wine; 75g perfume and .375 liter of toilet water; gifts to a value of £250.

If you return from a country outside the E.E.C. *or if the goods were bought in a duty-free shop on ship, plane or airport* the allowances are less: 200 cigarettes (or 100 cigarillos or 50 cigars or 250g tobacco); 1 liter of alcoholic drinks over 22% vol. (38.8DG proof) *or* 2 liters of alcoholic drinks not over 22% vol. *or* fortified *or* sparkling *or* still wine, plus 2 liters of still table wine; 50g perfume and .25 liter of toilet water; gifts to a value of £32. Note that tobacco allowances are double if you live outside Europe.

LISBON

Lisbon is a peculiarly beautiful city, descending from many hills to the great River Tagus to which, for centuries, she has owed her wealth and fascination. The city is a port, less busy now that international shipping has declined, but wharves, dockyards and warehouses still line the banks for some 16 km. (ten miles) from Xabregas to Belém. Terreiro do Paço or Palace Square, is the usual name for the Praça do Comércio (many of Lisbon's main thoroughfares have a second, more commonly used, designation). Surrounded on three sides by color-washed buildings above arcaded walks, in which are several Ministries, Terreiro do Paço is one of the most noble squares of Europe. The south side is lapped by the waters of the great river. Here, narrowing slightly below the Mar de Palha or Sea of Straw, the wide lagoon to the north east of the city, the river is tidal. In fact, the tides go on right up to Vila Franca de Xira, some 30 km. (18½ miles) up-river; this opening on the often turbulent waters gives a marvelous feeling of air and space to the huge square surrounding the superb 18th-century bronze equestrian statue of King José I, designed by Machado de Castro. The king, classically clad in a breastplate and plumed helmet, sits astride a splendid horse which has now weathered to a delicate green.

Many of the cross-river ferries sail from this square, as does the longer ferry route to Barreiro for the railway station, departure point of trains to the southern Alentejo and the Algarve. Although cargo boats still come up the river, the beautiful lateen-sail *fragatas,* or barges, which used to take merchandise from one bank of the river to the other, are now superseded by lorries going across the suspension bridge spanning the waters further down towards Belém. This bridge is slung high enough for the very largest liners to pass underneath even at high tide.

The center of the city is essentially 18th-century in architecture for it was rebuilt by the Marquis of Pombal, then Prime Minister, after the great earthquake in 1755. Pombal had been Portuguese Minister in London and this low part of the city, or the *Baixa,* is undoubtedly influenced by the Queen Anne architecture he had seen there. Straight rows of elegantly proportioned uniform house fronts, the surrounds of the windows and doors made of real stone (the country is rich in quarries of every kind) line the streets which are wide and straight with others crossing at right angles, so that it is a perfect example of early, and in this case very successful, town planning.

The district was to be given over to commerce and business and the streets were set apart for different trades. Thus, the Rua do Ouro, or Gold Street, still has a number of jewelers in it as well as a great many banks and the Rua dos Douradores, or Gilder's Street, is a reminder that Lisbon was noted for the fine gold leaf which was applied not only to church fittings, but also to furniture, ornaments and even the window shutters of palaces such as Queluz, which were picked out with real gold leaf.

Fortunately, the earthquake did not devastate the higher, older parts of the city—only the riverside area was totally destroyed—so visitors can still wander round the Castelo de São Jorge (Castle of St. George), whose foundations are lost in antiquity, and the medieval village which surrounds it, enclosed by great outer bastions. People still live and work here and it is a curious experience to walk along the narrow, twisting roadways between small houses alive with flowers, and gaily colored washing drying on struts above your head in the heart of the capital.

The other side of the great valley, which cleaves Lisbon from the Pombal statue at the top of the Avenida da Liberdade through the Rossio, the main square of the city, to the river, was also less affected by the earthquake. However, the ruins of the Gothic Convento do Carmo still standing above the Rossio are a perpetual reminder of what happened that morning of November 1, 1755. The splendid 17th-century Church of São Roque near the Bairro Alto, another maze of narrow streets, has survived to this day. Belém, to the west—where King José I and his court happened to be—was untouched by the earthquake, and here remains the superb Church of Jerónimos, the finest example of the late decorated Gothic style, called Manueline.

The Rossio, surrounded by austere 18th-century facades, is still the center of the city. Full of cafés and restaurants and a diminishing number of shops, it is a perpetually moving scene of dark-suited men talking together, lightly clad tourists and Lisboans scurrying about their business. Until comparatively recently, you would have seen bright yellow trams—which still run in the less busy parts of the town—bringing even more animation and color to the scene, as the flower sellers in the center of the square still do.

Today, public transport in the Baixa and up the Avenida da Liberdade is confined to motorbuses and taxis, which can be instantly recognized by their green tops. Private cars also fill up the roadways, perfect for 18th-century carriages and coaches, but not very adequate for today's automobiles. Indeed, the noble proportions of the Praça do Comércio have been much diminished by the presence of hundreds of cars parked in the large central space.

The Avenida da Liberdade, like the Champs Elysées in Paris, has been marred by apartment buildings devoted to offices and banks which are taking the place of its elegant private houses. But even so, you can still find enchanting examples of Victorian and art nouveau architecture scattered about the city on either side of the Parque Eduardo VII at the top of the Avenida da Liberdade. And just off the Rossio is one of the oddest railway stations in the world, with a Victorian-Moorish-Gothic facade: you have to go up in a lift or climb innumerable stairs to get to the trains, which are mainly suburban ones to Sintra and other surrounding towns.

With a little over 1,000,000 inhabitants, Lisbon is one of the smallest capitals in Europe. So, being cut by the great river to the south, spanned only in the last 20 years by the American-built bridge, Lisbon has always had to expand to the north, east and west. The way to the airport, for example, only a 20-minute run from the center of the city, is now built up by apartment houses; however, their color-washed facades, flower-filled balconies and natural stone embellishments give an air of solidity and a certain elegance to buildings which in other countries have so often begun to look rundown even before they have been completed.

Opening Up the World

Like all really ancient cities, the origin of Lisbon is surrounded by legends, some even saying that it was founded by Ulysses. It is an historical fact that Greeks traded along the Iberian coast and on very early maps Lisbon is called Olissibona. Later, the whole Iberian peninsula became a province of the Roman Empire. Even today, many of the roads in the country are clearly of Roman origin, and the enquiring traveler can seek out Roman bridges, some still used for their original purpose, particularly in the Alentejo. In addition, there are the well-known Roman remains at Conimbriga near Coimbra, and the Temple of Diana in Evora. The Romans were succeeded by the Visigoths who, it is believed, built the first cathedral in Lisbon.

When the Moors swept up from north Africa they not only improved the appearance of Lisbon, but also brought their sophisticated methods of irrigation to the dry lands of the peninsula, methods which are still in use today. Then came the Crusades: ships carrying English, German and Flemish crusaders to the Holy Land were driven ashore by a storm, and were persuaded by the young monarch Afonso Henriques, who had proclaimed himself king of Portugal in 1139, to stay and help him drive the Moors out of the southern part of his kingdom. So, in the summer of 1147, Lisbon was besieged and the Moors were driven southwards to the Algarve from which they were finally expelled a century later. The dedication of the Martires Church in the Rua Garrett in Lisbon recalls these foreign crusaders who fell in the battle against the Moors in Lisbon and were therefore regarded as martyrs for their faith.

In the 13th century what had been small settlements scattered over the country grew rapidly. Lisbon and Oporto in particular benefited from their position on the Atlantic coast which favored the development of maritime trade. These towns, with Braga, Coimbra and Lagos, were represented in the *Cortes,* or Parliament, which was at first held at Coimbra and then in 1256 moved to Lisbon, which thus became the capital of Portugal. At the end of that century the first Portuguese university was founded in Lisbon and shortly after transferred to Coimbra, thus making it one of the earliest European universities.

Under the Aviz dynasty, which started with the election by the Cortes of Dom João I (the previous king's illegitimate son) in 1385, Lisbon became the richest city of western Europe. Ships from all over the world brought wealth to her harbor, and it was towards the end of this century that a previous alliance of friendship with England was confirmed and strengthened by the signing of the Treaty of Windsor in 1386—a treaty which has never been abrogated and therefore remains the oldest alliance in the world. Almost a year later King John I married Philippa of Lancaster, the daughter of England's famous John of Gaunt, Shakespeare's "time-honored Lancaster." Their third son is known to history as Henry the Navigator who, from Sagres in the extreme southwest of Portugal, gathered information from seamen from all over the world and sent out expeditions which led, after the Prince's death, to the rounding of Cape Bojador in Africa and finally the discovery of the sea route to India by Vasco da Gama in 1498.

These historic discoveries were equal in their day to the American moon landing in the middle of this century. So enthralled was Manuel I that he built palaces and churches all over Lisbon with the huge profits of the sale of the first spices from India, giving his name to the extraordinary flowering of late Gothic architecture which is Portugal's contribution to European art—Manueline. The Jerónimos Church at Belém and the Abbey of Batalha to the north of the capital are the most remarkable examples of the style. Side by side with Christian symbols are coral, ropes, fruits, birds, fishes and exotic animals. The clergy devoted their wealth to beautifying their churches and chapels. Lisbon cathedral, Madre de Deus, and later São Roque, are examples of the flamboyant use to which the new found riches were devoted. Conceição Velha, which boasts a superb Manueline facade, was founded by Queen Leonore in 1498 as part of the Misericórdia hospice in Lisbon. Such charitable foundations, started so long ago, still exist in all major Portuguese towns and cities. Run by lay boards of local people, they have cared for the sick and helpless through the centuries; now that the state has, in most places, built modern hospitals just outside the towns, these old buildings have become homes for local old people.

The Spanish domination, when the Portuguese crown was united to the Spanish, lasted from 1580 to 1640. Strangely enough, the Spanish Armada against Great Britain sailed from the Tagus in 1588. After several abortive attempts to regain independence, a group of Portuguese nobles rose up and turned the usurpers out of the country and founded the Braganza dynasty. But during those 60 years Portugal declined in power, her overseas possessions were neglected by Spain, so that the Dutch were able to annex parts of the East Indies which were formerly Portuguese.

The Earthquake and After

The great earthquake of 1755 is still such a strong folk memory that even today few Portuguese wish to speak of that dreadful morning of All Saints Day, November 1. The churches were crowded when, towards ten

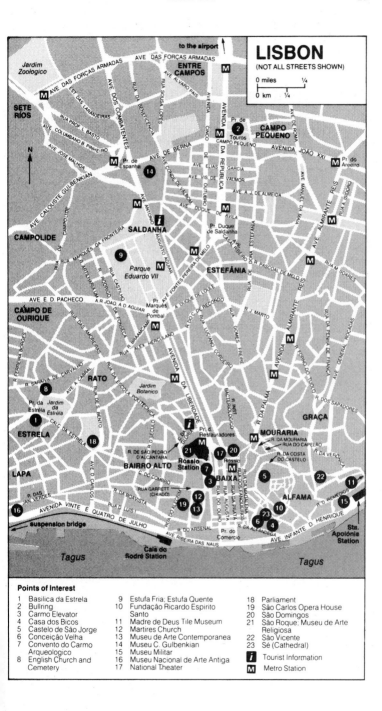

LISBON
(NOT ALL STREETS SHOWN)

0 miles ¼
0 km ¼

Points of Interest

1 Basilica da Estrela
2 Bullring
3 Carmo Elevator
4 Casa dos Bicos
5 Castelo de São Jorge
6 Conceição Velha
7 Convento do Carmo
    Arqueologico
8 English Church and
    Cemetery

9   Estufa Fria; Estufa Quente
10 Fundação Ricardo Espirito
    Santo
11 Madre de Deus Tile Museum
12 Martires Church
13 Museu de Arte Contemporanea
14 Museu C. Gulbenkian
15 Museu Militar
16 Museu Nacional de Arte Antiga
17 National Theater

18 Parliament
19 São Carlos Opera House
20 São Domingos
21 São Roque; Museu de Arte
    Religiosa
22 São Vicente
23 Sé (Cathedral)
i Tourist Information
M Metro Station

o'clock, around the beginning of Mass, a hollow rumble, swelling to a roar, shook the depths of the earth, which heaved up and all about. In the swaying churches, candles set fire to the hangings and woodwork. A strong wind was blowing, fanning the blaze and scattering the sparks. From the river, the ships' crews could see the church belfries rock and fall apart, the town burst into flames. The Tagus seemed to boil, first sucked down, then spewed up, overflowing its banks and sweeping all before it. Men, women, and children were crushed by falling stone, choked to death by dust and smoke and the hot gas from the cleft earth, or drowned in the tidal wave that swept along the dead together with the rubble.

Within six minutes, the lower part of the town was destroyed, and with it countless people. Panic-stricken, the survivors fled; plunderers mingled with the troops summoned to enforce order and give first aid. In the confusion that followed the earthquake, one man stood out, to sum up the task ahead: "Close the ports, bury the dead and succor the living." That man was Pombal, Minister of José I.

The emergency powers then granted to Pombal lasted well over 20 years. Clear-sighted and forceful, he mastered the panic, set the ruined city in working order, and, while the earth was still shuddering to a standstill, drew up his plan for Lisbon, wide of street and open to the cleansing sea air. He relocated the ruined streets downtown, and what was left of the old buildings on the river's edge. Sewers were dug, streets were built wide and at right angles. Around this modern downtown section, workmen were busy repairing fine family houses as best they could, rebuilding churches, putting up whole new quarters given over to industry: a glazed earthenware factory in the Rato, a silk factory in the Amoreiras, planted with mulberry trees for the silkworms. The Rossio was left in its place, slightly off-center in the new city plan, for the monks of São Domingos had refused to yield an inch of their lands.

The 19th century gave Lisbon gaslight, a monument to Pedro IV, and the royal palace of Ajuda, unfinished at the fall of the monarchy. The fashionable walk was the Passeio Publico, a fine tree-lined space behind the national theater built by Queen Maria II. Also a fashionable meeting-place, then as now, was the uptown street of the Chiado (Rua Garrett), lined with costly shops and coffeehouses, where men gathered at all hours of the day and night to talk politics and literature.

The assassination of King Carlos I and his elder son in 1908 led to the revolution of 1910, when the young King Manuel II went into exile and from thenceforth lived in England. Dr. Teofilo Braga, the historian, was made the first President of the newly-formed Republic. In the 1914–18 War, Portuguese troops fought in France alongside their British allies but from then until the arrival from Coimbra of Dr. Salazar in 1928, there was a constant succession of governments.

In 1940, 800 years after the foundation of Portugal and 300 years after the restoration of its independence from Spain, a Portuguese World Fair at Belém, on the banks of the Tagus, was held to celebrate this anniversary. It marked the beginning of the real effort to improve the run-down parts of Lisbon and Duarte Pacheco, then Minister of Public Works, started an extensive system of road building of which the excellent results still remain.

In 1966, the suspension bridge, 2½ km. (1 ½ miles) long, across the Tagus was opened. Fortunately the old ferries still run and you can take a trip across the river for a modest sum. This is a delightful way of seeing the city on its many hills, particularly at dusk, when the lights gradually pierce the quickening darkness, for Lisbon is too far south to have a lingering twilight. In stormy weather porpoises come up the river to shelter and play around the myriad little vessels that use the Tagus. On the south bank, a tall statue of Christ the King, alight in the night sky, blesses the town that has kept, through long years of changing fortunes, the unfailing beauty of its wide river. A lift goes to the summit revealing an unsurpassed view of the city.

After the bloodless revolution of 1974, Lisbon's monuments were apt to be covered with political graffiti or posters, though these have largely disappeared, their equivalent today being the ubiquitous faces of would-be political leaders left over from the last elections.

Exploring Lisbon

The airport is so close to the city that the traveler is in town before he knows it, driving under the branching trees of a shady park—the Campo Grande, where lovers stroll along the leafy paths, mothers take children to play, students from the nearby university sit reading on benches and row boats can be hired by the hour on the shallow lake.

Beyond the park, and between the tallest houses, the town still looks like a garden, for the housefronts are painted in flower-colors—pink and white, yellow and green. The traffic cops shelter from the sun and rain under umbrellas striped black and white, the town colors of Lisbon. This city has kept the thousand-year-old charm of the old Olissibona of the Moors: gardens flower in hidden courtyards, behind the wrought iron of the narrowest balcony, or the plate-glass front of the marble banks. Still to be heard at times are the plaintive notes of the *Gaita de Beiços,* a kind of Pan's Pipe which the knife grinders, who also mend umbrellas, play as they wheel their curious contraptions down the street, to warn householders to come out with their blunt knives to sharpen. Some of these men will also rivet broken plates.

Those who arrive by train from France or Spain will get off at the small and elegant Victorian station of Santa Apolónia, freshly painted in pink and black and white, and banked with green shrubs. It opens onto the docks, where the brown and red sails of fishing-smacks glide between cargo boats, river barges, and steamships. Beyond the port rise the church belfries and towers, the walls and steep streets of the old town, teeming with life as in the days of King Manuel, when tattooed sailors, colored slaves, and old women peddling charms crowded the wharves of the Ribeira. Caravelles are carved in stone on the walls. You will get a passing glimpse of the Casa dos Bicos, formerly the house of the Albuquerque family, with its diamond-cut front. The fresh sea air blows through the whole town, charged with the salty tang of dried fish hanging in the grocery stores, of dripping baskets of fish on the heads of *varinas,* from the 16 km. (ten miles) of dockyards between Lisbon and Belém, and from the river, glimpsed at every turning.

The traveler who comes from Spain on the southern highway can cross the Tagus to Lisbon by the bridge at Vila Franca de Xira, or by Europe's longest suspension bridge, midway between Belém and the Terreiro do Paço in Lisbon. As for the ferry-boats, they steam slantwise below the Mar da Palha (Sea of Straw) affording the traveler a slow, wheeling view opening full on Lisbon, much as the town appears in old etchings. A castle, towers, and church belfries still crown the swelling hills. So boundless to the sight is the roadstead behind the rocky spur of Cacilhas that the mouth of the river is lost to view. Narrowing his eyes in the murky sea-mist or the hazy sheen of heat, the traveler knows without being told that the stone outline in the far distance is the Tower of Belém.

Modern Lisbon

Those of us who love the old Lisbon, the *Lisboa Antiga* of Amália Rodrigues' haunting *fados,* are distressed by the high square buildings of the new quarters—sometimes painted in garish colors—at such odds with the graceful rise and fall of the low city skyline. Yet this modern Lisbon blends well with the old in a well-planned capital city of over a million inhabitants. Every day, big buildings take the place of town houses, decorated with turn-of-the-century stonework behind the then-fashionable palm tree.

Built almost overnight in the mid-20th century, the new Lisbon long kept her distance, spread out over countrified suburbs where flocks of sheep still grazed among the weeds of the new back lots, and tall apartment houses hemmed in small vegetable plots. There was room to spare. Fine, wide thoroughfares branched out from squares and circles, in planned perspectives. To fill the needs of a fast-growing town, the city planners, copying Pombal, undertook the wholesale building of long, straight streets of houses in the same pattern, keeping to the old roof tiles and the many balconies, at once filled with bird cages, flower pots, and hanging wash, that brought to the new quarters the old way of life.

Lisbon now has many airconditioned movie houses showing the same movies (original version with Portuguese subtitles) as everywhere else, shops, and restaurants, together with bowling alleys and snack bars, gathering places of young people very different from their elders. Experimental theaters proliferate owing to the generosity of the Gulbenkian Foundation. Whole city blocks have gone up, with a wealth of marble, trellised balconies and penthouses. For people of lesser means, there are low-cost apartment houses. The surge of new building has been roaring like a tidal wave in the direction of Estoril, crowning successive hills with high-rise blocks. Even so, there has been an acute housing crisis brought about by the long-term freezing of rents: with the fall in the value of money, people have not been moving out of their rented houses or apartments, and this has resulted in the large number of shanty towns on the outskirts of the city. However, the rent problem has been tackled and reasonable yearly increases are at last permitted.

Now that Lisbon has bridged the river, this modern city has spread to the south bank, where there is a series of working-class housing estates from which thousands of men and women commute daily.

Old Lisbon

Happily unlike most other cities, the Lisbon of the old days, the area from the Baixa to the Rossio, from São Roque to Graça, has not been flooded out by the new wave, but rather cleansed and embellished. The Pombaline housefronts of the Rua Augusta, the Rua do Ouro (Aurea),

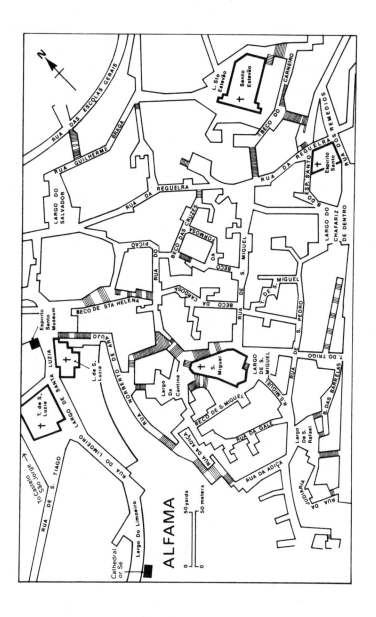

and the Rua da Prata—the Streets of Gold and Silver—have remained
untouched. The pavements of black and white mosaic work are in the formal checkered patterns of old; the square of the Rossio is inlaid in a ripple
of waves recalling the inrushing tidal wave of 1755; and strollers on the
Avenida walk over ships in full sail. They share a family likeness with the
streets of Rio de Janeiro.

The narrow pavements are always crowded by a colorful throng; the
hawker of lottery tickets, the blind street singer with his guitar, the fruit
peddler with his barrow and portable tin scales and many varieties of
goods laid out on the ground. Beggars have returned in force since they
are no longer obliged to live in special homes as they were before the revolution. Flowers are sold around the splashing fountains of Rossio. The
square has been cleared of streetcars, several cafés have given way to
snackbars, and within a few years fire gutted the church of São Domingos
and the National Theater. They have both been rebuilt and the church
now has an aluminum roof thrown over the calcined walls, making a superbly beautiful interior like a Piranesi print. The sun shines on the highest
hilltop, crowned by the old Castelo de São Jorge, lit up at night with green
floodlights, and overlooking the flashing neon signs of the town below.

A word of warning to the ladies—don't try to walk in town with thin-
soled or high-heeled shoes, at the risk of spoiling a good pair or twisting
an ankle on the pretty black and white mosaic-work of the steep streets.
Wear sensible flat heels, and walk in comfort and safety.

Cats, much loved by Lisboans, flit along garden walls, clinging to the
steep slope; they are of a breed which seems to be peculiar to Lisbon—
striped tabbies with long, pointed faces like those of the cats from Egyptian
tombs. The Portuguese people are somewhat oriental in their attitude to
animals: no one is willing to put down newborn puppies or kittens, so there
are a good many stray cats and dogs around; but people are kind and feed
them.

A smell of coffee wafts from huge cafés to mingle with a sharp salty
breeze. A crowd seethes and dawdles, at once busy and nonchalant. A play
of changing sunlight throws into strong relief the strange decor, giving
an impression of a city built like a theater. The Rossio, without a doubt,
is the heart of Lisbon, and as the people of Lisbon seldom seem to go to
bed early, the Rossio is as animated at midnight when the cafés close, as
at more conventional hours of the day. The Portuguese are not early risers
and many travelers are surprised when they find it difficult to get an early
breakfast in *pensão* or *residência* before catching a plane or a train. But
restaurants remain open until ten or eleven at night and you can always
get a meal until then.

Just off the Rossio, to the right of the National Theater, the great church
of São Domingos (closed lunchtime) was completely gutted in a terrible
fire some 30 years ago. Instead of restoring its former flamboyant 18th-
century decoration, a light aluminium roof, painted dark blue, was thrown
over the wide interior, and the calcined walls were left as they were. The
whole effect is of an etching by the 18th-century Italian, Piranesi.

The best shopping center has always been the Chiado, around Rua Garrett, though several city blocks in this area were devastated in the fire of
August 1988. Rebuilding is underway behind those facades that were
saved, but it will be a long time before the district fully regains its former
position as Lisbon's shopping showcase. Despite this, idlers still sit at the

marble-topped tables of the *Brasileira,* drinking black coffee and endlessly talking, as in the days of Eça de Queiroz. There are still the same crowds in the Churches of Loreto or the Incarnation, during Holy Week.

A little way to the north, in the Largo de São Roque, the church of the same name contains a wealth of good canvases and Baroque gold work, and the famous Chapel of St. John the Baptist, which was constructed in Rome by order of King João V and shipped to Lisbon. It is a symphony of lapis lazuli, agate, alabaster and mosaic. A small Museu de Arte Religiosa (Religious Art Museum) is next door.

Towards the river is the São Carlos Opera House, a lovely 18th-century building still used for its original purpose. Many of the visiting companies also give their performances at popular prices in the Coliseu, a huge circular hall accommodating 8,000 people, near the Rossio.

Throughout most of Lisbon, the rich and the poor live side by side, in an unthinking togetherness. In the flowered courtyard of a palace, children and cats play in the sun, the *varina* scrubs her fish basket at the stone fountain, the shoemaker sticks to his last under the stone coat-of-arms. Behind a peeling wall, a low door, there may well be big drawing-rooms with a wainscot of old glazed tiles, priceless East India Company china, and Germain silver, while in front of the palace of Abrantes, now the French Embassy, a former 17th-century convent shelters fishwives and dockhands in its cells and cloisters. Charcoal braziers, hanging wash, geraniums and green plants crowd the cracked stone of a fine old balcony; women gossip by a fountain as they wait in line to fill an earthenware jar with water; chickens scratch the earth, one leg tied by a string to the chair where a girl sits sewing. You will hear songs, the strumming of a guitar under the windows of a blind alley, a radio blaring in a tavern smelling of fried fish, the knife-grinder with his squeaky Pan's Pipes, the lilting cry of street peddlers—"Who wants figs?" "Sardines fresh from the sea," all the many homely village sounds that underlie the deep rumble of a big city. In the smart shopping streets you can often see elderly sable-clad men and women, the older country people who do not change into city clothes when they come up to town, but wear their usual black or dark suits and long skirts.

Strolling through Alfama

The best-known, the most beautiful, and the oldest part of the city is Alfama below the Castelo de São Jorge. The high ramparts of the Castle enclose moats in whose reedy waters swans and ducks feed, gardens on whose tended lawns peacocks fan open their tail feathers against the flowering bushes, and ivy-clad battlements alive with the cooing of white doves, while ravens are fenced in. A tall statue of Afonso Henriques in crusader's armor stands in the midst of a wide open space that overlooks the city and the river. Within the great outer walls of the Castle is a medieval village surrounding the parish church of the Holy Cross, in a tree-lined square with Michel's French Restaurant at one side. A rewarding walk can be taken through the busy, narrow lanes.

In order to reach the Castelo you'll have to clamber up through the old Alfama quarter. The less energetic should take a cab and stroll down. The streets are narrow, and the visitor has to pick his way between baskets of oranges and sardines, and groups of men gossiping in front of wine-shops. You will pass women carrying pitchers to the fountain and old men repairing fish nets. Sardines are usually grilled almost on the doorstep, and cats and geraniums sprawl on every balcony. Everyone seems to be busy making paper carnations for the June festivals. Old women try to sell you curious sweets and dried watermelon or sunflower seeds. There are tiny gardens no bigger than your hand, all overrun with urchins; church belfries are a-flutter with pigeons. Towards evening huge iron lanterns throw lacy shadows on the rough walls, and through narrow openings you catch a glimpse of the Tagus, busy with vast tankers and boats with red sails.

The Castelo to which you come is the Castelo de São Jorge today, but originally it bore the name of no Christian saint, for it was the Moorish Governor's palace, and his stronghold. They had picked their place well; visitors still plod up to it today for the magnificent view it affords over Lisbon and the Tagus. On the way you will arrive at the Miradouro de Santa Luzia, where a vine-shaded balcony offers an admirable view of river and rooftops. From the slopes of Alfama as far as the Tagus there arises a familiar and friendly city murmur, punctuated from time to time by the whistle of a tug-boat or the plucking of a guitar. On the walls of the little chapel here are paintings on glazed tiles: the capture of Lisbon by Afonso Henriques, and Terreiro de Paço before the earthquake.

Nearby, above Alfama, is a wide open space, filled with light from sky and water, called the Portas do Sol. All around the fine old houses of the rich stand side by side with white-washed cottages and noisy taverns. One of the finest was beautifully restored by a man of wealth and taste, the late Ricardo Espirito Santo, and furnished with his private collection of Portuguese works of art, found and brought home from all over the world. It is less a museum than a living 18th-century mansion. In a wing schools and workrooms have been installed to keep the old handicrafts alive.

Further down the slope the expertly reconstructed 12th-century Romanesque cathedral with extensive cloisters towers above the church of Santo António, built on the site where that popular saint was born. On the confines of the Alfama rises the Renaissance church and a large school, formerly a monastery, of São Vicente de Fora, whose tiled cloisters open on the chapel where all the Bragança kings, including Manuel II who died in England in 1932, are buried—no longer in glass-lidded coffins through which the embalmed bodies could be seen, but transferred to simple stone sarcophagi, except for the dynasty's founder who has been accorded Baroque pomp. King Carol II of Romania, exiled at Estoril, has been put provisionally to rest among the Portuguese monarchs. The burial chapel of Lisbon's Patriarchs nearby has room for only three more bodies.

Between the churches of São Estevão and São Miguel, antique dealers have set up shops, catering for all tastes and means. They lead downwards to the Terreiro do Trigo, and to the King's Fountain with its six outlets, one each reserved for noblemen, women, soldiers, sailors, servants and galley slaves.

The Bairro Alto and Mouraria Districts

To climb uptown to the Bairro Alto, take the Santa Justa elevator built, not by Eiffel as many claim, but by his protegé, Raul Mesnier. The openwork iron structure was a thing of beauty in its time, an eyesore in later years, and now is taking on an old-fashioned charm of its own. The footbridge on top overlooks the downtown streets of the Baixa, and leads to the silent ruins of the Carmo, past the Quinta Restaurant. The cable street-car of the Calçada da Glória, which takes off at the Restauradores, climbs up to the pretty tree-shaded terrace of São Pedro d'Alcántara, that overlooks Avenida da Liberdade below, and the Castelo São Jorge and the churches of Graça and Nossa Senhora do Monte beyond, each on its own hilltop.

For the more macabre-minded, a covered walkway has been built through the ruins of the fire of 1988, part of Rua Carmo and Rua Garret, and the disastrous effects to what was once the heart of sophisticated Lisbon can be seen at close quarters.

In the Bairro Alto, the streets are narrow but straight, like the threads on a loom. During the day, it rings with the noise of many crafts and smells of pitch and wood shavings and printer's ink from the newspaper presses. At night, another life awakens, that of bars and *fado* houses, some elegant establishments in vaulted cellars, with still-life paintings on the white-washed walls, some pleasantly rowdy taverns, some frankly folksy for the tourist trade.

The 18th-century houses of the Mouraria on the other side of the Rossio, long fallen into slums, are being cleared away by the city planners, and little is left of the once charming quarter, outside of sad old songs and the small chapel of Nossa Senhora da Saude, Our Lady of Health, who saved Lisbon from the black plague of 1576. Also left standing is the renowned Rua do Capelão, haunted by the ghost of the Severa, who was loved by a nobleman but took her pleasure with *toreiros* and ruffians, the unforgettable Severa who sang the *fado* as never before, comparable only to Amália Rodrigues. And to this day all *fadistas* wear black to mourn Severa.

Adegas Tipicas and the Fado

This is as good a time as any for a slight detour on the subject of *fado* and where to hear it. *Adega tipica* is the name given to the restaurant where you listen to *fado* singers and eat Portuguese specialties. Meals, however, are never obligatory at *fado* places and you can spend your time from after dinner till the small hours of the morning on local red or white wine or whatever other drink you favor while Portuguese guitars—which have eight or twelve strings and are slightly different in shape to the Spanish guitar which has six strings—accompany the *fadistas* and when the mood is especially good, one or other of the waitresses joins in and a kind of musical dialogue ensues made up entirely on the spur of the moment. Most authentic *fado* places are situated in the Alfama or Bairro Alto, the oldest parts of Lisbon, and are known by every taxi driver should you not remember the street. There are several other *adegas tipicas* in Lisbon but those mentioned in the Practical Information section at the end of the chapter have the best *fadistas* and the most romantic atmosphere.

Even if it's only for once in your lifetime, you must not fail to hear the *fado*. It's like eating ginger for the first time, or riding a roller coaster: *fados* are an experience to which you can't predict in advance your reactions. Underneath the customary external trappings—shawls, guitars, viols, gestures, posturings, melodic lines, the final great, wailing cry that is prolonged on the applause bursting forth with the last verse—*fado* can be either sublime or terrible, as replete with nuances as a rainbow. It must be straight out of the heart's depths, stark and untamed. *Fado* makes no pretense of trying to win you. True *fado*-lovers conscientiously shun the fake atmosphere of some of the fashionable spots where an attempt is deliberately made to cultivate a loose and flashy style that is the exact opposite of the true *fado*.

If you are seeking the real thing, you will find it only in surroundings that partake more of the folk spirit. And even so, it's all a matter of good luck, proper atmosphere, right mood. It depends on who's singing, who's listening. *Fado* is an art without virtuosity: it relies on instinct, the state of the nerves, a vibration rising out of the inmost being, a call from the heart. The least gifted performer may suddenly become possessed with the spirit, while the most renowned professionals can sometimes be utterly bereft of inspiration. So, whatever your experience or knowledge of *fado*— or your lack thereof—give it a fresh approach, search out for yourself the empathy that can be achieved spontaneously in a certain place with a certain *fadista* (in Lisbon, *fado* is pre-eminently a woman's art), and you will perhaps discover some hitherto unsuspected aspect of your own responsiveness. There's no mistaking the real thing when it occurs—it's frenetically alive and soul-wrenching, harsh and utterly unforgettable.

The best time to go to a *fado* café is after 11 P.M., though they may open around 9 or 10; most stay open to 3 A.M., some until dawn. Food is not a must, but two drinks per person usually is. In some of the less touristy ones, however, a dinner, followed by a long session of *fado,* makes a really memorable evening which will not cost an arm and a leg. There is normally a minimum charge, service and tax included.

The Tagus

It is to the Tagus that Lisbon owes her wealth and beauty, which would perhaps be heightened if a fine avenue ran the length of the water's edge. But the city is a port, the wharves crowded with landings for river barges, cargo, sailing, and ferry boats, fishing-smacks and steamships, together with dockyards and warehouses that line the banks from Xabregas to Belém. But between Terreiro do Paço and Cais do Sodré there is a breach on to the river, elsewhere to be seen only from a height in the distance though it remains a constant presence.

The Cais do Sodré, while insignificant in appearance, is fascinating for its animation and its incongruous mixture of fishwives, elegant Estoril commuters, and sailors of every nationality. In the bars you'll find people drinking pale ale or gin, and speaking English. From this quay you take the electric train for the Costa do Sol (the Estoril coast). The entire quarter depends on the port and on seagoing folk for its living.

At dawn the fishermen sell their catch by auction to the *varinas,* those lusty, dark-skinned fish vendors in wide black skirts whom you see trotting about the poorer parts of the city, carrying flat baskets of dripping fish on their heads. At dusk they come back to their own little kingdom, Madragoa, just behind the French Embassy—once the royal palace of Santos. The sovereigns used to come there by boat, with courtiers and musicians, to while away hot afternoons. And since it was tranquil and remote, fishermen from the north Atlantic coast made it their home. Some of them came from the village of Ovar—hence the nickname *varina.*

The people of Madragoa cling to their simple traditions and customs. *Varinas* wear gold hoops in their ears and necklaces with a heart or cross. When they have washed their baskets and set them to dry in the sun, they sit on their doorsteps to sew or gossip. Some of these thresholds belonged to old convents, for due to 19th-century anti-clericalism the neighborhood possessed so many unused religious establishments that working people moved into them. It would be hard to find places more active—and more vocal—than the cells and refectories of these ex-convents. But one of the charms of Lisbon is the abundance of such quarters as this, which retain the rustic and intimate character of a village.

On the nights of the Santo António or São João (St. Anthony's or St. John's Day) celebrations, no one expects to sleep in the poorer quarters. There is a continual round of processions, singing, and street dancing. Sometimes the British Ambassador or the French Ambassador stands on his balcony to watch the *marcha,* a noisy lanternlit parade that passes under the windows. For Madragoa is a neighbor of Lapa, the embassy quarter, and next to it comes Estrela, with its neo-classic basilica, separated by a park from the English church and cemetery, and the Parliament building. This is a garden spot of Lisbon, full of exotic flowers, peacocks, and enchanting houses.

Madre de Deus

It is worth following the river upstream, past the go-downs and the gantries and all the fascinating paraphernalia of the docks, to Madre de Deus. This beautiful church, built in the 16th century by Queen Leonor to house the relics of one of the Eleven Thousand Virgins of Cologne, had been badly damaged by the earthquake, and further spoiled in the following century by the construction of a nearby railway. The architect entrusted with the restoration of the Manueline church front based his blueprint on the retable of St. Auta, in the Museu de Arte Antiga, which portrays the arrival of the relics, greeted with great pomp by bishops and princes on the porch of the then-brand-new Church of Madre de Deus.

The church is renowned for its paintings (among which are portraits of King João II and his wife), its carved and gilded woodwork, and blue and white glazed tile panels of the life of St. Francis. There is an amusing panel in the chancel, of an avenue of trees which seem to go into the distance away from the onlooker, wherever he is standing.

In the cloisters of the neighboring convent is the Museu do Azulejo (tiles), tiles of painted and glazed earthenware of Arab origin, formerly in great use throughout Spain (and through Spain to Holland, where they are best made at Delft); this craft is today kept alive mainly in Portugal. A rich and varied display shows the growth and change of its style, from the first simple shapes and colors of the Moorish tiles to the modern Portuguese azulejo, now undergoing a wholesale rebirth.

Also in the Manueline style, in the Rua da Alfandega, the very fine porch in interlaced stonework is all that remains of the original Church of Conceição, given by King Manuel to his sister Leonor, widow of João II. It was there that she founded the Misericórdia, a hospice that, later, moved to São Roque, and still gives food and shelter to the poor, with the money raised principally from lottery tickets and a football pool. This

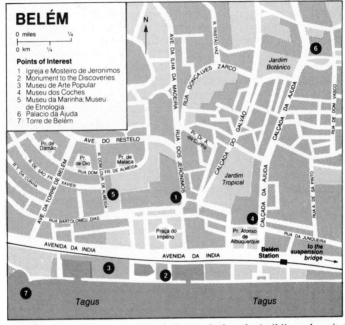

BELÉM

0 miles ¼

0 km ¼

Points of Interest

1 Igreja e Mosteiro de Jeronimos
2 Monument to the Discoveries
3 Museu de Arte Popular
4 Museu dos Coches
5 Museu da Marinha; Museu de Etnologia
6 Palacio da Ajuda
7 Torre de Belém

Misericórdia is now so extensive in its work that the buildings, hospitals, alms-houses, crêches etc. cover a large area in the center of the city.

Every town in the country has a Misericórdia, all stemming from the foundation of Queen Leonor's in 1498. In most places the hospital has been rebuilt on a more suitable site and the old buildings, usually with a lovely chapel, serve as homes for the aged.

The Museum of Ancient Art

The palace that was Pombal's keeps aloof and above the bustling port, on top of the great stone stairway that leads up from the wharves and the Avenida Vinte e Quatro de Julho. The palace houses the Museu Nacional de Arte Antiga (Museum of Ancient Art), and if at times the whole seems cramped in too narrow a space, the masterpieces are given ample room and set off by the best of lighting. The museum has on show old glazed earthenware, porcelain, sculpture, furniture, carpets, and silver and gold work, among which is the exquisite monstrance of Belém, made by the goldsmith and poet Gil Vicente out of the first gold brought back from Quiloa by Vasco da Gama. Also on display is the finest collection in the world of French silverware by the Germain brothers, whose masterly works of art were in other countries melted down or scattered as plunder during foreign and civil wars.

Most art lovers, however, go to the museum to see the paintings. The Flemish school (above all a nightmarish *Temptation of Saint Anthony* by Hieronymus Bosch); the German school (among which a Dürer and a Cranach are outstanding); and the early Portuguese paintings. From the art-less brushwork of Frei Carlos, one passes to the striking *Ecco Homo,* with the bleeding face of Jesus half hidden by his shroud. There are a few fine portraits: that of young King Sebastião, on whom coming misfortune had already cast its shadow; and that of an elegant nun in black and white, holding a coral rosary.

Above all, there is the many-paneled painting by Nuno Gonçalves (1460). Around São Vicente, patron of Lisbon, are gathered the people of Portugal, then on the threshold of her seagoing glory. There stand Henry the Navigator, King Afonso V, and the future King João II, together with their queens, among bankers and doctors, knights and captains, monks and priests, Jews, and sinners and beggars. Each man is a living portrait, and one cannot fail to be struck by the family likeness with the Portuguese of today. It is not merely a passage of time held still by Nuno Gonçalves, but the ever-renewed strain of a lasting race.

Jerónimos (Heronymites) Monastery, Belém Tower

It was a miracle that the earthquake of 1755 that rocked Portugal, and whose tremors were felt even in far Sweden, should have spared Belém, and thereby the royal family and the court.

Without the Jerónimos, without the Tower of Belém, little would be left in Lisbon of that strange, powerful, and original art form: Manueline architecture.

The Church of Santa Maria and the neighboring monastery were built on the beach of Restelo, at the very place where Vasco da Gama set sail and to which two of his three ships returned a year and a half later, half-wrecked, half the crew dead, but the holds full of spices and precious stones, and with the dream of his life come true: the discovery of the sea route to the Indies, and with it, the road to unimaginable riches.

Rarely has a monument stood so well for the spirit of its age. The fearful unknown of the high seas, the sailors' wonderstruck joy at the lushness of the tropics, the disturbing differences of race, all seem to have been worked into the stone, in a tangle of rope and shells and coral overlying the late Gothic structure. Through the south porch, facing the river, a dim watery light washes across the high nave; the noble finely decorated pillars seem so many towers of salty rock in a sea cave.

Near the tomb of Vasco da Gama is another dedicated to Camões, but the great poet died in poverty and was buried in a pauper's grave, his bones mingling with the bones of other outcasts. Nonetheless, his poetry echoes through the honey-colored arches. The royal tombs in the chancel rest on the backs of elephants, each different, with ivory tusks and wily little eyes. Be sure to see the great two-storied Manueline cloister, one of the finest in Portugal, behind the church, which can be reached from a door by the West Porch (closed at lunchtime). Stairs lead to the second story and on up to the broad walk right round the top, with lovely views over the Tagus and of the great church below. It was a Frenchman, Nicolas Chanterene, who adorned the west porch with the kneeling statues of King Manuel and his third wife Maria, daughter of a king of Spain.

Looking like an ivory chess piece, the Tower of Belém is carved with openwork balconies, a loggia, and turrets topped with domes. Originally out in the river, the bank has moved out to meet it. Long ago, it was the landmark that homecoming sailors strained to see from the lookout on the top mast of the sailing ship. Its beauty is a disarming front; behind the graceful stone lies hidden an armed fortress guarding the mouth of the river, with underground cells for prisoners. The terraces watched over by Our Lady of Safe Voyages have a sweeping view over the incoming and outgoing ships. Today, at the foot of the tower, the sails of pleasure craft flutter like white butterflies on the leaf-green waters of the River Tagus.

Around Belém

The monastery and the tower are reason enough to visit Belém. However, grouped around these twin witnesses of a splendid past, Belém has other points of interest, each well worth a visit.

The Monument to the Discoveries is modern, and looks, according to the angle from which it is seen, like a sword, a sail billowing in the seawind, or a *padrão,* the stone column carved with the arms of Portugal that was planted on each discovered land. It juts out into the river like the prow of a ship, and Prince Henry, caravelle in hand, sweeps seaward a whole people who for years worked with him towards the fulfilment of a country's dream: sailors and captains, soldiers and squires, priests and poets, caulkers and carpenters.

The lands and seas that Henry the Navigator caused to be discovered are mapped in many-colored marble on the star-shaped compass card that paves the open space beneath the monument.

The painted maps, the old instruments of navigation, the models of the caravelles and galleons, are all on display in the superbly arranged Museu da Marinha (Naval Museum), installed like the Museu de Etnologia (Ethnological Museum) within the precincts of the monastery. The royal barges and the cabins and fittings from the royal yacht are all fascinating.

The gold brought home from Brazil in the sailing ships was used in the gilding of the priceless carriages in the old royal riding school, now a museum, near the pink palace which is the official residence of the President of the Republic. The museum contains the largest carriage collection in the world, ranging from the leather coach of Philip II of Spain to the early 19th-century carriage that served to carry through Lisbon King Edward VII, Kaiser William and, in due course, Queen Elizabeth II. The richest, gilded and carved with mermaids and shells, trumpet-blowing allegories, and garlands of flowers, are the state coaches of the embassy which brought the Portuguese Ambassador and his suite from Rome in 1716.

The Portuguese people, fishermen, sailors, peasants and soldiers, to whom the country owed its wealth, have their Museu de Arte Popular (Museum of Folk Art) in Belém. Carvings in wood and cork by the shepherds of the Alentejo, wrought iron from the backwoods of Trás-os-Montes, *ex-votos* by the fishermen of Sesimbra, pictures of birds and flowers and boats in colored tinfoil by the fishermen of Nazaré, handmade lace and red cross-stitch on shirts and bed linen, crocheted bedspreads, earthenware, rugs made of plaited rush and checkered fur, bedecked harnesses for mules, carved yokes for oxen; everything to give a touch of beauty to the hard and humdrum life of everyday. The sight of this true handicraft will go far to prevent the visitors being trapped into buying tourist trash.

Then, for the visitor who wants to make the full rounds of the Portuguese world, there are the Tropical Gardens, to the right of the monastery. There, he will breathe in the heavy tropical odors of trees and fruit and flowers from the jungles of Brazil and Angola. And just beyond is the huge palace of Ajuda, still partly unfinished as on the day young King Manuel abdicated in 1910. The State Rooms, used for official receptions, are shown and include enchanting examples of Victorian decoration and a room furnished with Saxe porcelain, chairs, tables and mirrors. The Library contains an outstanding collection of manuscripts and incunabulae.

Edward VII Park and the Gulbenkian Foundation

So far we have spent most of our time downtown and along the banks of the Tagus. Striking up from the Rossio runs the Avenida da Liberdade, the "Champs Elysées" of Lisbon. This long tree-lined avenue repays a gentle saunter, with perhaps a stop for an ice-cream at one of the parlors on the left. The avenue isn't what it once was, for it has become the stamping ground of oil and insurance companies, houses most of the major airline offices, has several cinemas and is very noisy indeed. But the open-air cafés and the variety of statues and central trees almost make up for the din.

At the top of the Avenida da Liberdade is the square dedicated to Pombal. With one hand on the mane of a bronze lion, Pombal stands on the top of his monument, looking down over the city he re-ordered, and no doubt wondering at the swirling traffic under his nose. Behind him lie the cool, ordered, green depths of the Parque Eduardo VII, Edward VII park. This is also the area of the main hotels, from the old-established Ritz to the new Meridien. The new hotels have brought a series of shopping malls and other facilities which are a definite plus to the Lisbon scene.

In the park are the Estufa Fria and the Estufa Quente, a Cold House and a Hot House, covering several acres with exotic trees, plants and bushes under high roofs of slats and glass.

From here it is an easy walk to the Gulbenkian Foundation just off the Praça de Espanha. This complex is one of the most attractively designed museums in the world; which is not really surprising when one considers the resources and talent that were available to the builders. The Museum itself houses the priceless collection of the Armenian oil tycoon, including silverware, paintings and sculptures, Persian miniatures, coins and carpets and Lalique jewelry. It is not a collection that is strong in massive accumulations in any one field, but relies upon a few superb examples in each to make its impact. It is quite one of the pleasantest museums to wander through as well, since it was custom built for the collection, and most of the rooms have views out over the park that surrounds the complex. There are two halls for the annual music and ballet festivals, a large gallery for temporary exhibitions and open-air performances take place in the park in summer. The library is open for research, and there is also a handy bar and canteen. The Modern Gallery has an exceptionally good self-service restaurant.

Epilogue

Lisbon is neither the biggest nor the most beautiful city in Europe. However, it does have a special quality. It is a capital city that has managed to combine the features of a seaside location with an atmosphere of being out in the country, and the coolness of the hills is but a few minutes away. Resting lightly on these hills overlooking the estuary with huge tankers awaiting their turn to go into the Lisnave shipyards at Cacilhas on the south side and the great river that widens above the city into the Mar da Palha, Lisbon never conveys a feeling of heaviness. Any Sunday during the summer months May through September you can chug along by boat for two pleasant hours on the Tagus, sightseeing Lisbon and the river banks while comfortably seated. Departures are from Terreiro do Paço ferry station at 2:30 P.M.; but check times at the tourist office.

There is an infinite variety of pleasant walks to be taken. In whichever direction you may choose to go, you will come out on some new and delightfully unexpected view of the city and the river. The most ordinary-appearing street presents an unfailingly lively passing scene, and there is always something going on.

Lisbon still retains an extraordinary number of art nouveau buildings—apartments, individual houses and shop fronts. In the older parts of the city many of the facades are covered with patterned and even pictured, glazed tiles, the latter often depicting the trade carried on in the shop, such as screws and tools on an ironmongers in the Rua de São Paulo. Traffic police are kind to cars with foreign plates, but there are a large number of very reasonable car parks in the city.

In and around Lisbon there are all the pleasures of the oceanside to be enjoyed. The electric train along the Sun Coast puts the beach within ten minutes' distance from Cais do Sodré station. Sea sports are available all along the way to Cascais (plus tennis, golf, and horsebackriding). On the opposite shores of the Tagus (a ferry-boat trip always makes a nice ride), the gleaming expanse of the beaches of Caparica can be reached by ferry from Belém.

If blissful solitude is your fancy, you will find it among the dunes of Guincho beyond Cascais. And you can go fishing along the Portuguese coast at all times of the year without a license.

Should you simply want to commune with nature, a bus will whisk you off to Monsanto's wooded slopes (camping, swimming pool, outdoor restaurants, panoramic view). Thirty to 40 minutes in your car, or by train from Rossio station, will bring you to Sintra's gardens, to the Serra and its untamed fastnesses, perfect for walking, picnicking, a bit of mountain-climbing . . . or even shopping for antiques in Sintra village. From Easter-time on through the early autumn, Vila Franca do Xira (29 km., 18 miles, by motorway) stages a tauromachian spectacle, complete with processions of mounted *campinos* (cattle-herders), farriers, bullfights and bullfighters.

If time is limited and you can't possibly visit other parts of the country, the mere fact of being in Lisbon will give you a complete idea of all the diversified aspects of Portuguese life. The Portuguese genius is domestic and small-scale. People matter, so civilized living and concern for others, goodwill and politeness are the norm and not the exception.

PRACTICAL INFORMATION FOR LISBON

WHEN TO COME. Spring and fall are, naturally, the favorite times for visiting Lisbon, though the nostalgic, lingering warmth of early November is hardly less appealing. July and August are not unpleasantly hot (there is always a cooling breeze at night), but these are the peak tourist months. There are plenty of places to go in the fall and winter evenings.

Nights in Lisbon are cool. Even during the warmest months the breeze stirs towards evening, and it's advisable to take a scarf or some light wrap when you venture forth after sunset. In fact, in this city that lies like a great amphitheater under a benign sky, the wind is the reason that you see really very few outdoor terraces, although many restaurants offer splendid views from glassed-in terraces. It is a memorable experience to enjoy dinner from some vantage-point where you can watch the ruins of the Carmo gradually silhouette themselves against the sky, or see the shining lights of Rossio come on in the velvety distance; and it is safer to walk about Lisbon at night than it is in most other big cities.

TOURIST OFFICES. There are Portuguese Tourist Offices at Palácio Foz, Praça dos Restauradores (tel. 363314), at Avenida António Augusto de Aguiar 86 (tel. 575091), and at the airport (tel. 893689).

TELEPHONE CODE. The code for Lisbon is (01), but it is specifically for calling the city from the provinces, and should not be used for Lisbon or its environs when calling *from* Lisbon or its environs.

HOW TO GET AROUND. By Train. Avoid the subway unless absolutely necessary. The service is limited and it is one of the favorite haunts of pick-pockets.

Frequent and excellent, one-class electric trains leave from Cais do Sodré Station, traveling along the Costa do Sol to Cascais, beyond Estoril. Fare 100$00 single to Estoril or Cascais. Trains for Sintra leave from Rossio Station. Tickets bought on the trains are subject to a huge surcharge.

By Tram. The tram service is one of the best in Europe and this is the most amusing and enjoyable way of getting about in Lisbon. Books of 20 tickets, at half the price charged on the trams or buses, can be bought at Cais do Sodré and other terminals, as can a Tourist Pass for a little over 1,000$00. You will have to produce your passport. This is good for 7 days on all trams, buses, and subways. The *Carris* (Lisbon Transport Company) produce an excellent map and booklet, with a comprehensive list of all the bus and tram routes.

This very efficient tramway system is a fascinating survival, built by British engineers at the end of the last century. Two of the many hills are the steepest that have ever been worked by trams, anywhere in the world, without a rack or cable. These are on route 28, Graça/Prazeres and on route 12, Martim Moniz/São Tomé. If you want to see a large part of the city, take the former from the Largo da Graça to Prazeres, or route 18 from Praça do Comércio to Ajuda.

By Bus. These also provide a good city service—see *Carris* booklet. There is a special bus service from the airport to the city center called *Linha Verde* (the Green Line).

By Cable Car. These link some of the higher, and lower, parts of Lisbon. The Gloria rises from the Restauradores to St. Pedro de Alcantara; the Lavra from the east side of the Avenida da Liberdade to the Campo

Martires da Patria; and the Bica from the Calçada do Combro to the Rua da Boavista. The vertical lift of Santa Justa links the Rua do Ouro with the Carmo Square.

By Taxi. Taxis are plentiful and cheap. Cabs, with green roofs, start at 80$00. In fact, for two to four people, going by cab will probably be the cheapest way to travel. Tip about 5–10%. Taxi fare from the airport into Lisbon is about 500$00.

Chauffeur-driven cars are also available, with good drivers. Inquire at car-rental firms—see under *Useful Addresses*—or from your hotel porter.

By Boat. Ferryboats for Cacilhas leave from alongside the Praça do Comércio and Cais do Sodré, the latter taking cars; for Barreiro, from the Estaçao do Sul e Sueste, just off the Praça do Comércio; for Trafaria, and Caparica, from the Estação Fluvial de Belém.

It's worth taking the 10-minute trip to Cacilhas and from there the bus marked Cristo Rei to the statue of Christ in Majesty. This offers a stunning view of Lisbon, the bridge, and, on a clear day, the castle at Sintra.

HOTELS. The Lisbon hotel scene within recent years has been much improved by the opening of new establishments and the modernization of others. Nevertheless, for the peak season, reservations should be made well in advance.

Deluxe

Meridien, Rua Castilho 149 (tel. 690900). 318 rooms with bath. Lisbon's latest luxury hotel, all tiles, glass and shine; rooms can be a bit on the small side. Sauna, garage, 3 restaurants. AE, DC, MC, V.

Ritz, Rua Rodrigo da Fonseca 88 (tel. 692020). 300 rooms with bath. Top hotel in town. Rooms are large and stately. Garage, good parking; grill room, excellent restaurant; airconditioned. Above the Eduardo VII Park, with magnificent view over the city. AE, DC, MC, V.

Sheraton, Rua Latino Coelho 1 (tel. 575757). 388 rooms with bath. Pool, rooftop restaurant; parking difficult; airconditioned. A small section of the hotel, **Sheraton Towers**—28 rooms, all with bath—is set aside as an even more expensive enclave. AE, DC, MC, V.

Expensive

Alfa, Ave. Columbano Bordalo Pinheiro (tel. 722121). 375 rooms with bath. Restaurant *Pombalino* highly recommended. 10 minutes from center. Pool, disco, garage, good parking. AE, DC, MC, V.

Altis, Rua Castilho 11 (tel. 560071). 219 rooms with bath. International Bridge Club, garage, large car park. AE, DC, MC, V.

Avenida Palace, Rua 1° de Dezembro 123 (tel. 360151/9). 95 rooms with bath. Public rooms all gilt, crystal chandeliers and plush furnishings; very old-fashioned; breakfast only. Central, convenient for shopping. AE, DC, MC, V.

Lisboa Plaza, Travessa do Salitre 7 (tel. 363922). 93 rooms with bath. Snack bar. Off Ave. da Liberdade. AE, DC, MC, V.

Tivoli, Ave. da Liberdade 185 (tel. 530181). 344 rooms with bath. Top-floor restaurant with terrace and superb view; garage; central. Deluxe-standard, charging slightly less than top rates. Highly recommended. AE, DC, MC, V.

Moderate

Britania, Rua Rodrigues Sampaio 17 (tel. 575016). 30 rooms with bath. Breakfast only. AE, DC, MC, V.

Diplomatico, Rua Castilho 74 (tel. 562041). 90 rooms with bath. Modern rooms; terrace with panoramic view; private parking. AE, DC, MC, V.

Dom Manuel I, Ave. Duque de Avila 189 (tel. 561410). 60 rooms with bath. Breakfast only. AE, DC, MC, V.

Eduardo VII, Ave. Fontes Pereira de Melo 5 (tel. 530141). 120 rooms with bath. Bar and roof restaurant, overlooking the city. AE, DC, MC, V.

Fenix, Praça Marques de Pombal 8 (tel. 535121). 116 rooms with bath. More suitable for families; grill room serving Spanish dishes. Strategically located at top of Av. da Liberdade. AE, DC, MC, V.

Florida, Rua Duque de Palmela 32 (tel. 576145). 108 rooms with bath. Family-type hotel; breakfast only. AE, DC, MC, V.

Lisboa Penta, Ave. dos Combatentes (tel. 7264629). 592 rooms with bath. Pool; all modern amenities. Two restaurants, garage, good parking. Located 10 minutes from center, near U.S. Embassy. AE, DC, MC, V.

Mundial, Rua D. Duarte 4 (tel. 863101). 146 rooms with bath. In commercial sector. AE, DC, MC, V.

Novotel, Ave. José Malhoa (tel. 7266022). 246 rooms with bath. Pool; parking, restaurant grill. Recommended although not central. AE, DC, MC, V.

Principe Real, Rua da Alegria 53 (tel. 360116). 24 rooms with bath. Attractive rooms; pleasant, relaxed atmosphere; breakfast only. AE, DC, MC, V.

Rex, Rua Castilho 169 (tel. 682161). 40 rooms with bath. Small in size, great in comfort, with first-class restaurant and easy parking. AE, DC, MC, V.

Tivoli Jardim, Rua Julio Cesar Machado 7 (tel. 539971). 119 rooms with bath. Fine annex to the Tivoli, with good restaurant, snack bar, pool, tennis, parking. AE, DC, MC, V.

Inexpensive

Avenida Alameda, Ave. Sidónio Pais 4 (tel. 532186). 27 apartments, all with bath.

Avenida Parque, Ave. Sidónio Pais 6 (tel. 532181). 40 rooms with bath. Breakfast only; next door to Avenida Alameda hotel.

Berna, Ave. António Serpa 13 (tel. 779151). 154 rooms with bath. Breakfast only. Garage. Near the bullring and Gulbenkian Foundation. AE, DC, MC.

Borges, Rua Garrett 108–110 (tel. 3461951). 99 rooms with bath. Old-fashioned charm and good modern service; very popular with Portuguese and others up from the country; on main shopping street. No parking. AE, MC, V.

Botanico, Rua da Mãe de Agua 16 (tel. 320392). 30 rooms with bath. Central. Breakfast only. AE, DC, MC, V.

Capitol, Rua Eça de Queirós 24 (tel. 536811). 50 rooms with bath. Snack bar. Solid comfort. AE, DC, MC, V.

Da Torre, Rua dos Jerónimos 8 (tel. 630161). 52 rooms with bath. In suburbs very near Jerónimos Church, Ethnological, Coach, Folk Art and Naval Museums and Ajuda Palace. AE, DC, MC, V.

Dom Afonso Henriques, Rua Cristóvão Falcão 8 (tel. 8146574). 33 rooms with bath. Breakfast only; not central. DC, MC.

Dom Carlos, Ave. Duque de Loulé 121 (tel. 539071). 73 rooms with bath. Breakfast only, sauna, garage. AE, DC, MC, V.

Duas Nações, Rua da Vitória 41 (tel. 320410). 66 rooms, most with bath. Breakfast only; central, in business sector.

Embaixador, Ave. Duque de Loulé 73 (tel. 530171). 96 rooms with bath. Disco. AE, DC, MC.

Excelsior, Rua Rodrigues Sampaio 172 (tel. 537151). 80 rooms with bath. Off Ave. Liberdade. AE, DC, MC, V.

Flamingo, Rua Castilho 41 (tel. 532191). 39 rooms with bath. Very pleasant, friendly. AE, DC, MC, V.

Impala, Rua Filipe Folque 49 (tel. 558914). 26 apartments with bath and kitchenette for up to 4 people. AE, DC, MC, V.

Infante Santo, Rua Tenente Valadim 14 (tel. 600144). 27 rooms with bath and balcony. Breakfast only; comfortable residential hotel, but not central.

Jorge V, Rua Mouzinho da Silveira 3 (tel. 562525). 49 rooms with bath. Pleasant; breakfast only; near Ave. da Liberdade. AE, DC, MC, V.

Lis, Ave. da Liberdade 180 (tel. 563434). 63 rooms, half with bath. Breakfast only; good value and central. AE, DC, MC, V.

Metropole, Rossio 30 (tel. 369164). 50 rooms, half with bath. Breakfast only; noisy, central. AE, DC, MC, V.

Miraparque, Ave. Sidónio Pais 12 (tel. 578070). 101 rooms with bath. Obliging staff; located beside Eduardo VII Park. Be sure to garage your car overnight, as some readers have complained of thefts when left outside.

Presidente, Rua Alexandre Herculano 13 (tel. 539501). 59 rooms with bath. Nice rooms, breakfast only; central. AE, DC, MC.

Principe, Ave. Duque d'Avila 201 (tel. 536151). 56 rooms with bath. AE, DC, MC.

Reno, Ave. Duque d'Avila 195 (tel. 548181). 51 rooms with bath. Breakfast only. AE, DC, MC, V.

Roma, Ave. de Roma 33 (tel. 767761). 264 rooms with bath. Good value, with pool, sauna, shops, garage, snack bar, and rooftop restaurant with view over city. Not central. AE, DC, MC, V.

Senhora do Monte, Calçada do Monte 39 (tel. 862846). 27 rooms with bath and balcony. Top floor restaurant with lovely view; in old town. AE, DC, MC, V.

Suiço Atlantico, Rua da Gloria 13 (tel. 3461713). 88 rooms, most with bath. Breakfast only; central. AE, DC, MC, V.

Vip, Rua Fernão Lopes 25 (tel. 578923). 54 rooms with bath. Breakfast only. AE, DC, MC, V.

PENSIONS. By U.S. or U.K. standards the estalagems, residências and albergarias of Lisbon offer excellent value for money. There are many, and among the best are—

York House (M), Rua das Janelas Verdes 32 (tel. 662544). 68 rooms with bath or shower; and in annex at no. 47 in same street, 12 rooms with bath. Mansion in own garden, but up long flights of steps; good simple food, highly recommended. AE, DC, MC, V.

Albergaria Pax (I), Rua José Estevão 20 (tel. 561861). 30 rooms with bath. Breakfast only; away from center.

Nazaré (I), Ave. António Augusto Aguiar 25 (tel. 542016). 32 rooms with bath. Breakfast only. AE, DC, MC, V.

Pensão Astoria (I), Rua Braamcamp 10 (tel. 521317). 67 rooms, most with bath. Central.

Pensão Dom Sancho I (I), Ave. da Liberdade 202 (tel. 548648). 20 rooms with bath. Breakfast only; central.

Residência America (I), Rua Tomás Ribeiro 47 (tel. 531178). 60 rooms with bath. AE, DC, MC.

Residência Canada (I), Ave. Defensores de Chaves 35 (tel. 538159). 40 rooms with bath. Breakfast only.

Residência Capital (I), Ave. Elias Garcia 87 (tel. 767330). 22 rooms with bath. Breakfast only.

Residência Imperador (I), Ave. 5 de Outubro 55 (tel. 574884). 43 rooms with bath. Breakfast only.

São Mamede (I), Rua Escola Politecnica 159 (tel. 663166). 25 rooms, most with bath. Old mansion; breakfast only.

Mansão Santa Rita (P), Ave. António Augusto Aguiar 21 (tel. 547109). 15 rooms with bath.

Pensão Casa de Sao Francisco (P), Ave. da Republica 48B (tel 766600). 24 rooms, most with bath. Breakfast only. Good value.

Pensão Castilho (P), Rua Castilho 57 (tel. 570822). 19 rooms with bath. Breakfast only. Good value.

Pensão Ninho das Aguias (P), Costa do Castelo 74 (tel. 860391). 16 rooms, 6 with bath. Breakfast only; superb view, no parking.

Residência Horizonte (P), Ave. António Augusto Aguiar 42 (tel. 539526). 52 rooms with bath. Breakfast only.

CAMPING. Monsanto Parque Florestal, off the autostrada to Estoril and Cascais.

YOUTH HOSTEL. Rua Andrade Corvo 49 (tel. 532696).

RESTAURANTS. The Portuguese prefer to do most of their eating at home, whether they're *en famille* or entertaining friends, which may be a reason why every so often even really good restaurants become unpredictable; returning in pleasurable anticipation of previously excellent food, one can be faced with disappointment. In the main, however, very good meals can be had at many places. All restaurants, even the luxury establishments, have to show their price list displayed outside.

Restaurante-Cervejaria (beer-restaurants) are small, modest eateries, very inexpensive; but beware, for they cook with garlic and the heavy pungent olive oil *azeite,* and the taste and odor are not to everyone's liking.

Incidental intelligence: except in the smartest restaurants or in those with a show or dancing, you can always ask for *Vinho da Casa* and suffer no loss of face. The house wine is always easy on your palate and a bottle of red or white comes at a reasonable price. Always check your bill. Tables do not need to be reserved, except in the expensive places. Several Lisbon restaurants close on Sundays. But cafés are open.

Portuguese love children and you can take a child of any age into any restaurant—they will be very welcome and charged half price up to 8 years old and younger children can eat from your dish. Some of the inexpensive places list half portions. Two can share a dish, as portions are often too large for one.

Expensive

António Clara, Ave. da Republica 38 (tel. 766380). On ground floor of large, rescued, art-deco house (upstairs is a private club). Highly recommended for both atmosphere, food—some of the best in Lisbon—and an interesting wine list for anyone who wants to experiment with fine vintages at reasonable prices. Highly trained staff. Private parking. AE, DC, MC, V.

Aviz, Rua Serpa Pinto 12B (tel. 328391). This restaurant was saved from the ruins of the old Avis hotel by the staff. Decor like a set for *The Merry Widow,* with turn-of-the century atmosphere to match, and unique washrooms. Closed Sat. dinner, Sun. AE, DC, MC, V.

Casa da Comida, Travessa das Amoreiras 1 (tel. 685376). Imaginative cuisine in delightful setting round small, courtyard garden; attentive service; very fashionable, so book in advance. You'll have to look attentively for the door in! Closed Sat. lunch, and Sun. AE, DC, MC, V.

Casa de Leão, Castelo de São Jorge (tel. 875962). Top quality, lunches and teas only. AE, DC, MC, V.

Clara, Campo dos Martires da Patria 49 (tel. 557341). Attractively converted—and slightly out of center—townhouse; elegantly bourgeois interior; shaded patio garden for summer; helpful, professional service. Closed Sun. AE, DC, MC, V.

Gambrinus, Rua Portas de Santo Antão 23 (tel. 321466). Worth the trouble to find if you enjoy shellfish and smoked things. Comfortable, with entry through small bar. Always open. AE, DC, MC, V.

Michel's, Largo de Santa Cruz do Castelo 5 (tel. 864338). Genuine French food; inside the outer walls of St. George's Castle, with easy parking. Closed Sat. lunch and Sun. AE, DC, MC, V.

O Terraco, Ave. da Liberdade (tel. 530181). On the top floor of the Tivoli hotel, this restaurant offers a panoramic view of Lisbon. The food is excellent, especially from the grill; the service is unobtrusively attentive. AE, DC, MC, V.

Pabe, Rua Duque de Palmela 27A (tel. 535675). English-type pub with restaurant behind; near Pombal Square. Highly recommended. Always open. AE, DC, MC, V.

Tagide, Largo da Academia 18–20 (tel. 320720). Tasty local specialties—like pork and clams—at top prices; recently renovated. Closed Sat. lunch, Sun. AE, DC, MC, V.

Tavares Rico, Rua Misericórdia 35 (tel. 321112). Superb cuisine and wine list, a rival of the Aviz, with turn-of-the-century setting. Closed Sat. lunch, Sun. AE, DC, MC, V.

Moderate

António, Rua Tomás Ribeiro 63 (tel. 538780). Local clientele tells its own story; usually full. AE, DC, MC, V.

Arameiro, Travessa Santo Antão 21 (tel. 367185). Always crowded, noisy and lively, and no wonder—the specialty, chicken on the spit, is truly superb. Always open.

Bodegon, Praça Marquês de Pombal 8 (Tel. 529155). Enjoy real Spanish dishes in comfort in this, the grill room of the Spanish-owned Hotel Fenix. Always open. AE, DC, MC, V.

Comida de Santo, Rua Engenheiro Miguel Pais 39 (tel. 663339). Attractive bohemian atmosphere and decor, the Brazilian food served here is excellent. Gets very busy late on. AE, DC, MC, V.

Como Sequeira, Rua Gustavo Matos Sequeira 30 (tel. 677433). Near British Institute.

Cozinha d'el Rey, Rua Castilho 169 (tel. 682161). In Rex Hotel, first-class food in a most attractive setting. Always open. AE, DC, MC, V.

Escorial, Rua Portas de Santo Antão 47 (tel. 363758). Spanish cuisine in formal surroundings; shellfish specialties. In side street off Rossio; always open. AE, DC, MC, V.

Gondola, Ave. Berna 64 (tel. 770426). The only place in town where you can eat under a canopy of leaves, and of course you pay for the privilege; rich Italian dishes. Opposite Gulbenkian Foundation. Closed Sat. dinner, Sun. MC, V.

Kamikaze/Vento de Deus, Rua Filipe Folque 23 (tel. 524264). Near Sheraton Hotel. Without doubt the best Japanese restaurant in town. Authentic atmosphere, Japanese newspapers on hand; friendly and helpful staff. AE, DC, MC, V.

Nanking, Rua Sousa Martins 5A (tel. 521746). Chinese food; fairly reasonable. Always open.

O Alexandre, Rue Vieira Portuense 84. Cheerful place. Near Jerónimos. Closed Sat.

O Manel, Parque Mayer (tel. 363167). Fine Portuguese cooking. Always open.

Petite Folie, Ave. António Augusto de Aguiar 74 (tel. 521948). Very acceptable French cooking. Garden terrace in summer. AE, DC, V.

Sagitario, Rua de Belém 10 (tel. 645687). Near Jerónimos. Excellent food. Closed Sun.

Sancho, Travessa da Gloria 8–16 (tel. 369780). Off Ave. Liberdade. Good food and service; rustic decor. Closed Sun. AE, DC, MC.

Solmar, Rua Portas de Santo Antão 108 (tel. 360010). Fish idle about in a large tank while you make your choice. Serves wild boar, venison, game. Always open. AE, DC, MC.

Sua Excelencia, Rua do Conde 40 (tel. 603614). The dining out experience of Lisbon. No menu, the flamboyant owner describes the mouthwatering dishes in several languages. The most esoteric menu in the capital; personalized attention. Reservations a must. AE, DC, MC, V.

Telheiro, Rua Latino Coelho 10A (tel. 534007). Enormous helpings, and no one minds if you ask for half portions. Crowded for lunch as it's near new business area, but tranquil for dinner. Always open. DC, MC.

Toni dos Bifes, Ave. Praia da Vitória 50 (tel. 536080). Small cozy bistro specializing in steaks. Closed Sun.

Inexpensive

Atinel Bar, Cais dos Cacilheiros (tel. 372419). Off Praça do Comércio. The only restaurant in Lisbon right on the Tagus—get a table by the picture windows. Outdoor eating too. Very friendly service. Always open.

Bom Apetite, Travessa da Gloria 20 (tel. 360101). Cheap, plentiful meals with friendly service. Closed Sun.

Bonjardim, Travessa Santo Antão 11 (tel. 324389). Chicken, freshly spit roast, also excellent barbecued suckling pig turned golden brown on a spit in this modest restaurant in a narrow, short street beside the main post

SEE PAGE 23

office in Restauradores, where there is underground parking. To get in, go earlier or later than 1 or 8 o'clock—the peak times—and this holds true for all small eating places. AE, DC, MC, V.

Cervejaria Trindade, Rua Nova da Trindade 20C (tel. 323506). Good-value food; with cave-style wine cellar and a garden. Always open.

Ceuta, Ave. da Republica 20C (tel. 531305). Snack bar specializing in delicious cakes which also serves meals. Always open.

Colombo, Ave. da Republica 10H (tel. 549225). Lunches, teas, dinners, plus a huge variety of good cakes. Open daily to 10 P.M.

Dionysos, Rua de Belém 124 (tel. 640632). Greek food near Jerónimos; recommended. MC, V.

Farah's Tandoori, Rua de Santana à Lapa 73 (tel. 609219). Delicious curries and friendly service. Closed Tues. MC, V.

Forno da Brites, Rua Tomás Ribeiro 73 (tel. 542724). Practical food; staff helpful to tourists. Closed Sat. AE, DC, MC, V.

Great American Disaster, Praça Marquês de Pombal 1 (tel. 521266). On first floor of Varig building. Best hamburgers in town. Always open. AE, DC, MC.

Hong Kong, Rua Camilo Castelo Branco 23 (tel. 538665). Good Chinese food and prompt attention. AE, DC, MC, V.

Ladeira, Ave. Marques de Tomar 33 (tel. 772520). Serves a variety of food, with half portions if you can't manage a whole—these are enough for two. Open mid-day to 10:30 P.M. Closed Fri. dinner, Sat.

Laurentina, Ave. Conde Valbom 69 (tel. 760260). Run by Mozambiqueans, so food is somewhat exotic. Closed Sun.

Lira de Ouro, Rua Nova de São Mamede 10 (tel. 663306). Central, good food, very reasonable. Closed Sun.

Noite e Dia (Night and Day), Ave. Duque de Loulé 51A (tel. 573514). Good value and always crowded; self-service. Open 12–3, 6–10.30. Closed Sun. AE.

O Funil, Ave. Elias Garcia 82A (tel. 766007). Plentiful portions, served in simple surroundings. Popular with office-workers.

O Guardanapo, Rua Padre António Vieira 4A (tel. 691016). Excellent snack bar. Closed Sat., Sun.

A Quinta, at top of Elevador de Santa Justa (tel. 365588). Serves Portuguese, Russian, and Hungarian specialties. View and pleasant ambience. No parking; closed Sat. dinner, Sun. AE, MC.

O Rafael, Rua de Belém 106 (tel. 637420). Between Jerónimos and Coach Museum, with pretty patio for outdoor meals. Good value. Closed Mon.

Ribadouro, On corner of Rua do Salitre and Ave. da Liberdade (tel. 549411). Bar-restaurant specializing in seafood. Bar snacks are particularly good. AE, MC, V.

Torio, Rua Tomás Ribeiro 38 (tel. 553655). Portuguese food in snack bar and at tables. Half portions served. Closed Sat.

Venha Cá, Rua Nova da Trindade 10C (tel. 321986). Drinkable house wine and reasonable food; country decor. Closed Sun.

Xangai, Ave. Duque de Loulé 20B (tel. 557378). Like *China* Chinese cooking and is also near U.S. Library. Always open.

Snack bars and Pastelarias. These are all over town. The names may mislead you—don't expect milk shakes and sundaes, as you would at home. The following are some of the leading ones.

Bernards, Rua Garrett 104. For tea addicts.

Brasileira, Rua Garrett. Beautiful old-style coffee shop with a life-size statue of national poet Fernando Passoa sitting at one of the sidewalk tables.

Pasteleria de Belém, Rua de Belém, near Jerónimos. For coffee and the delicious Belem *pasteis* (pastries) served hot with cinnamon and sugar.

Snack Ritz, Rua Castilbo 77. Below Ritz Hotel. Excellent light meals at counters, but expensive.

Tofa, Rua d'Ouro 177. Good coffee and tasty tidbits. Downtown.

Tascas. Pub and bistro combined. **Farta Brutos,** Travessa Espera 20, in Bairro Alto. Good food. AE.

Porto de Abrigo, Rua de Remolares 16. Smart tasca, with excellent crab and duck dishes. Closed Sun.

Sardinha Assada, Cais do Sodré 2. Very convenient, and you can eat as much as you wish for a reasonable price.

NIGHTLIFE. Lisbon nightclubs in general don't rank in the international class. New ones open, fairly new ones fold; it's unpredictable. If you are after a more atmospheric evening, you should seek out one of the Adega Tipicas (see below), both to hear *fado,* and for a less expensive time. Discos are everywhere and open and shut unexpectedly.

Ad Lib, Rua Barata da Salgueiro 28–7 (tel. 561717). Smart and respectable. AE, DC.

Banana Power, Rua de Cascais Alcantara 51 (tel. 631815). Also one of the most respectable and chic nightclubs. MC.

Barracuda, 12 Rua da Misericórdia (tel. 368649). Not exclusive; exotic but with a firm grip on reality.

Loucuras, Ave. Alvares Cabral 37 (tel. 681117). Young, fashionable spot.

Plateau, Escadinhas de Praia 18 (tel. 665116). New and fashionable.

Stones, Rua do Olival 1 (tel. 664545). Chic and respectable. DC.

Whispers, in Commercial Center at Ave. Fontes Pereira de Melo 35 (tel. 575489). Also chic and respectable. AE, MC.

Port Wine Institute, Rua São Pedro de Alcantara 45. Excellent place for a pre-dinner drink, an attractive spot despite its formidable name. Open 10 A.M.–midnight. Closed Sun.

Adega tipica. This is the name for the places where you listen to *fado* singers and eat Portuguese specialties. Meals are not obligatory, you can spend your time from after dinner to the small hours in the morning supping wine or whatever other drink you fancy. The singing seldom starts before 10 P.M. Most are in the Bairro Alto. Reservations advised for dinner.

A Severa, 51 Rua das Gáveas (tel. 364006). A bit touristy—beware souvenir-sellers. Closed Thurs. AE, DC, MC.

Fado Menor, Rua das Praças 18 (tel. 671856). Intimate and pleasant. A few steps from *Senhor Vinho's.* AE, MC, V.

Lisboa a Noite (Lisbon by Night), 69 Rua des Gáveas (tel. 368557). Don't be put off by the name, it's not *that* touristy, and the owner, Fernanda Maria, is an outstanding singer. Expensive. Closed Sun. AE, DC, MC.

Luso, Travessa de Queimada 10 (tel. 362889). One of the long-established fado places. Good value. Closed Sun. AE, DC, MC.

Machado, Rua do Norte 91 (tel. 360095). Typical bustling tourist place, where guests are invited to join the staff dancing round in a circle with the lighted candles from their tables. Closed Mon. AE, DC, MC.

Marcia Condessa, Praça da Alegria 38 (tel. 367093). With the usual dramatic trappings.

O Faia, 54 Rua da Barroca (tel. 326742). Soft, husky voices, soul-searing melodies, all the trimmings. Also folk-dancing and singing. Reasonable in price. Open to 3.30 A.M. Closed Sun.

Parreirinha de Alfama, Beco do Espirito Santo 1 (tel. 868209). Informal, with excellent food, in the oldest part of Lisbon.

Senhor Vinho, Rua do Meio-a-Lapa 18 (tel. 672681). Smart, in diplomatic district. AE, DC, MC, V. Closed Sun.

Timpanas, 24 Rua Gilberto Rola (tel. 672431). Where the real heart of Lisbon beats. Prices reasonable. Closed Mon. MC.

Dinner-dance. There are a few pleasant dinner-dance restaurants, sometimes with floorshows.

Choupana, Estrada Marginal, São João do Estoril (tel. 2683099). Newest and smartest, with live band and good food. Expensive; parking; out of Lisbon. AE, DC, MC, V.

Monaco, at Caxias on the road to Estoril (tel. 2432339). Looks over the sea; is expensive, and has very good food. Parking. AE, DC, MC, V.

O Porão da Nau, Rua Pinheiro Chagas 1D (tel. 571501). Has the best band to dance to. Expensive but not exclusive. Open 11 P.M.–4 A.M.

CONCERTS, OPERA AND BALLET. Opera and ballet are performed from late January through June at the São Carlos and São Luis Theaters. Concerts and recitals, as well as ballet, take place at the Gulbenkian Foundation October through June.

BULLFIGHTING. Try to attend at least one night performance of a *tourada,* or bullfight, especially if it's the kind called *antiga portuguesa,* complete with carriages, tricorns, and 18th-century embroidered costumes. In Portugal, the bull is not killed, and it's a great show whatever the quality of the actual fight, and even if you're not an ardent *aficionado.* The horses are as highly trained as polo ponies and are not touched by the bull. Starts at Easter, and continues through Oct. in the Campo Pequeno, generally on Thursdays and Sundays.

SIGHTSEEING DATA. Museums are usually open daily, except Mondays and public holidays, 10–5, but double check the times on the spot. Some close for lunch. Entrance fees are between 150$00 and 300$00.

Aquario (Aquarium), Ave. Marginal, Dafundo. Good selection of Atlantic fish; sea lions. Trams: Alges, Dafundo. Buses: 12, 23, 29, 50. Adm. free Wed. Open weekdays and holidays 12–6, Sun. 10–6; closed Mon.

Arqueologico (Archeology), Largo do Carmo. Medieval sculpture set in spectacular ruined Gothic church. Tram: Carmo. Santa Justa elevator. Closed for lunch, 12–2.

Basilica da Estrela, Praça da Estrela. Important monument; splendid view of Lisbon and the Tagus from the dome; room-sized Christmas crib is worth seeing, on payment of a small fee. Trams: Estrela, Prazeres. Buses: 9, 20, 22. Closed for lunch, 1–3:30.

Castelo de São Jorge (St. George's Castle), covering high hill to east of center. Wonderful views of city and River Tagus. Picnic facilities. Adm. free. Bus 37.

Estufa Fria (Cool House), in the grounds of Parque Eduardo VIII. Magnificent tropical plants; *Estufa Quente* (Hothouse) has superb orchids in winter. Tram: Carmo. Buses: 2, 3, 4. Adm. 48$00. Open 9–sunset.

Fundação Ricardo Espirito Santo (Museum of Decorative Arts), in an old palace at Largo das Portas do Sol. Well worth a visit: part museum, part training center for craftsmen, here you can see some of the best rugs, silver, furniture and lamps ever made in Portugal. Antiques are sent from all over the world for repair; many of the *Ritz Hotel* furnishings came from here. Tram: Graca. Bus: 37. Closed for lunch, 1–2:30.

Igreja de Madre de Deus (Church of the Mother of God). A masterpiece of Portuguese Baroque, with fine tiles and gilded woodwork. Tram: Poço do Bispo. Buses: 13, 18, 42.

Igreja e Mosteiro de Jerónimos (Jerónimos Church and Monastery), Praça do Império, Belém. The Manueline style at its best. Be sure to see the double cloisters. Trams: Algés, Dafundo. Buses: 12, 27, 28, 29, 43, 49. Closed for lunch, 12:30–3.

Jardim Botanico (Botanical Gardens), Rua Escola Politecnica. Trams: 24, 29, 30. Bus: 15. Adm. free. Closed Sat. and Sun. Sept. through Apr.

Jardim Zoologico (Zoo), Parque das Laranjeiras, Estrada de Benfica. The animals look contented in their large enclosures, only the polar bears resent the sun. Dogs and Cats Hotel, strange Pet's Cemetery, Children's Zoo with miniature houses and small animals. Picnickers are welcome; several snackbars and restaurants, and even Bingo. Buses: 15, 16, 26, 31, 34, 41, 46. Adm. 200$00, 100$00 for children 7–10 years. Open 9–sunset.

Lisbon Aqueduct. Entrance in Calçada da Quintinha, Campolide. Open July, Aug., Sept., Oct. on Sat. and Sun. 10 A.M.–5 P.M. The Mae das Aguas, the great 18th-century covered reservoir in Praça das Amoreiras, is open every afternoon except Mon.

Museu da Agua (Water Museum), Rua do Alviela 12. Closed for lunch.

Museu de Arte Contemporânea (Museum of Modern Art), Rua Serpa Pinto. 19th- and 20th-century Portuguese painting and sculpture. Tram: Prazeres. Closed for lunch, 12:30–2.

Museu de Arte Popular (Museum of Folk Art), Ave. Brasilia, Belém. Rich and eloquent presentation of provincial art and lore. Trams: Algés, Dafundo. Buses: 12, 29, 43. Closed for lunch, 12:30–2.

Museu de Arte Religiosa (Museum of Religious Art), next to São Roque Church, Largo Tríndade Coelho. Ecclesiastical vessels, goldsmiths' work, vestments. Trams: 24, 29, 30. Bus: 15.

Museu do Azulejo (Tile Museum), Rua da Madre de Deus. In the cloisters and convent of Madre de Deus. Trams: 13, 18, 42. Closed for lunch.

Museu Calouste Gulbenkian (Gulbenkian Foundation Museum), Ave. Berna. In two side-by-side sections, classical and modern. One of the world's most impressive galleries, its collection including masterpieces by world-famous painters, items bought from Leningrad's Hermitage Museum in 1929–30, a noted Middle Eastern collection, coins, bronzes, glass and carpets. The Modern Gallery has a fair amount of perishable stuff—the Gulbenkian is in the laudable business of supporting talent; but it's still worth visiting. The custom-designed rooms look out over attractive modern gardens. Good restaurant in Modern Gallery; snackbar. Buses: 30, 41, 46, 56. Adm. 40$00. Open Tues., Thurs., Fri., Sun. 10–5; Wed. and Sat. 2–7; closed Mon.

Museu da Cidade de Lisboa (City of Lisbon Museum), in magnificent Palácio Pimenta, Campo Grande. Buses: 1, 7, 33, 36, 50. Closed 1–2.

Museu dos Coches (Coach Museum), Belém. Finest collection of coaches and carriages in the world, from late 16th-century to Victorian, in beautiful 18th-century riding school. Trams: Belém, Algés, Dafundo. Buses: 12, 27, 28, 29, 43, 49. Open 10–1, 2:30–5:30.

Museu de Etnologia (Ethnological Museum), Praça do Império, Belém. Prehistoric, Greek and Roman relics. Trams: Algés, Dafundo. Closed 12–2. Buses: 29, 43.

Museu Dr. Anastácio Gonçalves, Ave. 5 de Outubro 8. Collection in private house, largely Chinese porcelain. Buses: 1, 21, 36, 38, 44, 45, 49.

Museu da Marinha (Naval Museum), Praça do Império, Belém. Fascinating for naval buffs—ship models, royal uniforms, barges. Next to Planetarium. Trams: Algés, Dafundo. Buses: 29, 43. Adm. free Wed. Open 10–5.

Museu das Marionetas (Marionette Museum), Largo Rodrigues de Freitas 20. Bus: 37.

Museu Militar (Military Museum), Largo dos Caminhos de Ferro. Armor and weapons from 15th-century to present. Tram: Poco do Bispo. Buses: 9, 13, 17, 35. Open 10–4.

Museu Nacional de Arte Antiga (Ancient Art), Rua das Janelas Verdes. One of Europe's great collections of paintings, ceramics, silver and tapestries. Fine Portuguese primitives; famous 15th-century polyptych by Nuno Gonçalves, *Triumph of St. Vincent;* works by Hieronymus Bosch, Frans Hals, Holbein, Dürer, and many other Dutch, Spanish and Italian painters. Germain brothers' silver table service made for King João V and gold church vessels. Tram: Alcantara. Buses: 27, 40, 49 or 54. Snack bar with pies, sandwiches, etc.

Museu Nacional do Trajo (Costume Museum), Largo São João Baptista 2, Lumiar. In lovely 18th-century Palmela Palace, with superb gardens. Restaurant (expensive). Buses: 1, 7, 36. A way out in the suburbs, but possible to use a taxi and get it to wait (as long as you aren't having a meal too). Closed for lunch 1–2:30.

Museu do Teatro (Theater Museum), beside Costume Museum, see above. Fascinating if slightly provincial theatrical exhibits, very well displayed in restored old palace. Same transport and times as the Costume Museum.

Palácio de Ajuda (Ajuda Palace), Largo da Ajuda. Early 19th-century palace with fine rooms, good furniture and paintings, etc. Tram: Ajuda. Buses: 14, 40, 42.

Planetarium, Praça do Império, Belém. Shows, mostly at weekends, announced on board outside. Buses 29, 43.

São Vicente (St. Vincent's Church), Largo de São Vicente. Impressive building with exquisite wall tiles in the cloisters. The Braganza royal Pantheon is off the cloisters. Tram: Graça. Closed for lunch, 1–3.

Sé (Cathedral), Largo da Sé. Rebuilt 13th-century structure with a notable iron grill in the cloister. Tram: Graça. Bus: 37. Closed for lunch, 12–2:30

Torre de Belém (Belém Tower), Ave. da India. Marks the place from which the tiny caravelles sailed to unknown shores. Collection of arms and armor. Buses: 29, 43.

TOURS AND EXCURSIONS. Among the Lisbon travel agents offering every kind of travel assistance including tours are: *Capistranos,* Ave. Duque de Loulé 47A (tel. 542973), whose coaches pick up passengers at several hotels for day and overnight tours; *Citirama,* Ave. Praia da Vitória 12B (tel. 575564), who operate daily sightseeing tours with taped commentaries in eight languages; *Marcus and Harting,* Rossio 50 (tel. 369271).

SPECIAL EVENTS. Easter. Clam-hunt—on Maundy Thursday and Good Friday crowds are to be seen on the beaches north of Sintra, digging and scraping clams off the rocks, to be put into a tasty clam soup at the end of the day. By all means join in, although the tradition is fading nowadays. Just remember to use a knife or some other strong blunt instrument.

June. International Fair at Belém. The *Feira Popular,* a fun fair, is open in summer near Entrecampos. 13, 24 and 29: merry noisy festivities in old Alfama, to honor the *Santos Populares,* Saints Anthony, native son of Lisbon, John, Peter and Paul. The costumed evening parade held yearly on the eve of June 13, each *bairro* in fierce, enthusiastic competition with the others, lasts well after midnight, and is followed by celebrations till dawn. Small taverns are packed, people jostle, dance and shout in the streets, whilst the unmistakable odor of grilling sardines wafts under paper lanterns swinging over winding alleyways.

SHOPPING. Shopping in Lisbon can be both rewarding and fun as there are still large numbers of individual shops and very few big stores. The smartest are in and around the Rua Garrett, or the Chiado, as it is always called—although the fire of August 1988 devastated part of this area—and the Baixa, the area between the Rossio and the River Tagus, but there are also excellent shops in the new residential districts towards the airport. All handmade goods, such as leather handbags, shoes, gloves, embroidery, basketwork and fine book-binding are to be found at very reasonable prices. Most Lisbon shops are open from 9–1 and 3–7, and shut at 1 P.M. on Saturday.

The huge blue-and-pink Amoreiras commercial center contains a multitude of shops selling clothes, shoes, food, Atlantis crystal, Vista Alegre china etc., as well as a hairdresser, restaurants and ten cinemas. The center is open till midnight.

Jewelry and Antiques. It is easy to get old clocks and watches and antique jewelry well repaired: the former at *António Couto,* Rua Sampaio Pina 52, near the Ritz Hotel, while jewelry can be reset as well as mended at *António da Silva,* Praça Luis de Camões 40. The last-named shop and *Barreto & Gonçalves,* Rua das Portas de Santo Antão 17, have the widest

selection of antique jewels and silver for sale. There are many modern jewelers' shops in the Baixa, and *Sarmento,* Rua do Ouro 251, has an exceptional collection of the gold and silver filigree work which is so characteristic of Portuguese craftsmanship.

It is exceedingly rare to find a bargain in Lisbon antique shops, which
are concentrated in the Rua Escola Politecnica, Rua Dom Pedro V, Rua
da Misericórdia and the Rua do Alecrim (really one street although it has
four different names). The flea market, the *Feira da Ladra* in the Campo
de Sta. Clara is behind the Church of São Vicente. It is held all day on
Tuesdays and Saturdays.

Leather Goods. Shoe shops are all over the city but, as Portuguese
have very small feet, it is often difficult to find the larger sizes ready-made.
However, all the better shoe shops will undertake to have shoes made to
measure. Beautiful handbags and fine luggage can be found at *Galeão,* Rua
Augusta 196, and *Casa Canada* at 232 in the same street also has a large
selection. Gloves are usually sold or made to order in specialist shops in
the Rua do Carmo and the Rua do Ouro. *Coelho,* Rua da Conceição 85,
is excellent for leather belts and will make up your own material into leath-
er-backed belts. This street, one of the cross roads in the Baixa, is famous
for buttons, wools, cottons and all sewing materials.

Porcelain, Pottery and Tiles. *Vista Alegre,* in the Largo do Chiado
18, produces the finest porcelain in the country. Their factory near Aveiro
was founded in 1824 and you can buy perfect reproductions of the original
table services and ornaments as well as modern designs. They also sell fine
glass. Portugal is full of clay, and local craftsmen turn out delightful bowls
and plates for daily use, as well as the glazed pictorial tiles for which the
country is famous. *Viúva Lamego,* Largo do Intendente 25, has the largest
selection of tiles in Lisbon. Not only are their prices very competitive, but
the staffs are most helpful, and their stock vast. The *Fabrica Sant'Anna,*
Rua do Alecrim 95, near Chiado, also sells hand-painted tiles and pottery
in traditional patterns. The green pottery cabbage leaves, plates and tureens from Caldas da Rainha are to be found in all the handicraft shops.

Embroidery and Basketwork. Being light in weight, both embroidered goods and baskets make wonderful gifts for airborn travelers. The
Casa Regional da Ilha Verde, Rua Paiva de Andrade 4, just off Rua Garrett, has beautifully embroidered table linen and blouses from the Azores.
Tito Cunha at numbers 179 and 246 Rua do Ouro, specializes in the same
type of goods from Madeira. Arraiolos carpets, hand-embroidered in wool
in traditional or modern patterns, are to be found at *Quintão,* Rua Ivens
30. Baskets and basketwork of every kind can be bought in the markets
which are all over Lisbon, selling fruit, vegetables, fish, meat and poultry,
but are only open until 2 P.M. One of the best specialist shops for baskets
is *Cestos,* Ave. Duque d'Avila 8B, which is at the top of the city off the
Ave. da Republica.

Food and Wine. The major exports of Portugal are port wine and cork.
The latter, from the great cork forests in the Alentejo, does not make attractive presents, though you will find small boxes and zinc-lined buckets
called *tarros,* with fitting lids which will keep ice frozen for hours. Port

wine comes from the vineyards of the Douro river above Oporto, and can be bought at any of the good wine shops and grocers around the city. One of the best is next to *Vista Alegre* in the Largo do Chiado, and if you want to sample several varieties go to the *Solar do Vinho do Porto,* Rua São Pedro de Alcantara 45, which is run by the trade and where you can sample over 100 varieties of Port.

There are several delicatessens in the Baixa selling fine foods, including the delicious regional cheeses as well as a big range of wines. Those from the different regions are particularly good, not only *Dao,* which is well known, and *Setúbal,* a generous wine from south of Lisbon, but also *Redondo, Borba, Evel* and *Vidigueira* from the Alentejo, *Lagoa* from the Algarve, *Nabantino* from Estremadura, *Cartaxo* from the Ribatejo, *Bairrada* and the *Vinhos Verdes,* or green wines, which are slightly sparkling, from the north.

The best fresh chocolates are to be found at *Benard's* at the top of the Rua Garrett. They also stock the many varieties of dried and crystallized fruits including Elvas plums, which are a feature of the country, and serve light lunches and teas.

All these firms are reliable for sending goods abroad and the *Centro de Turismo e Artesanato,* Rua Castilho 61, not only stocks a wide variety of typically Portuguese products, but they will also despatch goods abroad by air or sea freight even if bought elsewhere.

A Final Round-up. *Ramiro Leão,* Rua Garrett 83, is an excellent store for all household goods, materials, baby clothes, etc.

There are good hairdressers and barbers all over town, such as *Bruna,* Largo de São Carlos 8 (tel. 363821). *Adelina* at Rua Garrett 61 (tel. 321982) is also very up-to-date as is *Hair,* Galerias Ritz, Rua Castilho 77A, Shop 5 (tel. 577855), *Tabot,* Ave. António Augusto de Aguiar 19-CV-D (tel. 532755), is smart and very reasonable in price. They all do facials and beauty treatments. Only the leading hairdressers make appointments—in the others clients wait their turn.

For books in English go to the *Livraria Britanica,* Rua de São Marçal 170, at the side of the British Institute, with a very large stock of paperbacks and hardbacks. *Bertrands, Sá e Costa* and the *Diario de Noticias* bookshops are all in the Rua Garrett and have foreign as well as Portuguese books. If you break your glasses or lose your prescription, *Ramos e Silva,* Rua Garrett 63, are excellent and quick for repair work or filling new orders.

SPORTS. For further details of sports facilities ask at Tourist Offices. **Tennis:** courts near Campo Grande or at Cruz Quebrada can be reserved at the Club Internacional de Ténis, Rua Professor Sousa Camara 193 (tel. 682084). There are also tennis courts, as well as a **swimming** pool and a 9-hole **golf** course in a picturesque natural setting at the Lisbon Sports Club, Carragueira, near Belas, 15 minutes' drive from Lisbon.

Clay-pigeon shooting at the beautiful Monsanto Club, 10 minutes' drive from town. **Horse-riding** rates are reasonable.

Skindiving: divers interested in the Portuguese underwater flora and fauna, or those who feel up to coping with a live lobster, should contact the Centro Portuguese de Actividades Subaquáticas, Rua do Alto do Duque 45 (tel. 616961), which organizes tourist expeditions to the coast

at Sesimbra, Arrábida, Algarve, in which non-members can also partici-
pate.

Fishing is done from the shore by hired rowboat or by specially
equipped large boats for big game fishing (swordfish, tuna, or big-eyed
tuna off Madeira). There is fresh-water fishing, for trout, rainbow trout
and large-mouthed bass, which was imported a few years ago from America.

NEWSPAPERS. Lisbon has a large number of weekly and daily newspapers, of which the *Diario de Noticias* is the most comprehensive. The
Anglo-Portuguese News is an English-language weekly covering local and
general news.

USEFUL ADDRESSES. Embassies. *American,* Ave. das Forces Arma-
das (tel. 7266600); *British,* Rua São Domingos à Lapa 37 (tel. 661191);
Canadian, Rua Rosa Araújo 2 (tel. 563821). **Travel Agents.** *American Express,* Star Travel Service, Ave. Sidónio Pais 4A (tel. 539841/50/71), and
at Praça dos Restauradores 14 (tel. 362501); *Wagons Lits/Cooks,* Ave. da
Liberdade 103 (tel. 361521), and at the Ritz Hotel, Ave. Rodrigo Fonseca
88 (tel. 680632); *Wasteels Expresso,* Ave. António Agusto de Aguiar 88
(tel. 579180).

Car Hire. Most international firms have offices at the airport: *Avis,*
Praça dos Restauradores 47 (tel. 361171); *Europcar,* Ave. António Augusto Aguiar 24 (tel. 535115); *Hertz,* Ave. 5 de Outubro 10 (tel. 579027); *In-
terRent,* Praça dos Restauradores 74 (tel. 366751); *Travelcar,* Ave. Fontes
Pereira de Melo 6 (tel. 578006).

Chauffeur Driven Cars. *Auto Estrela,* Ave. João Crisóstomo 65 (tel.
534331); *Castanheira,* Ave. João Crisóstomo 87 (tel. 540744); *Olivauto,*
Ave. João XXI, 12D/E (tel. 880178); *Turigal,* Rua Fialho Almeida 36E
(tel. 542846).

Automobile Clubs. *Automobile Club of Portugal,* Rua Rosa Araujo 24
(tel. 563931); *Touring Club of Portugal,* Ave. da Liberdade 258 (tel.
561011).

Pharmacies. See any paper for the day's list of pharmacies open that
night or Sat. P.M. or Sun.; if closed the pharmacy has a notice giving the
nearest that are open.

Hospital. *British Hospital,* Rua Saraiva de Carvalho 49 (tel. 602020),
(night tel. 603785), with English-speaking staff, for both in- and outpatients.

Lost Property. Should you lose or mislay sunglasses, cameras, gloves
or whatnot, try checking at the municipal *Governo Civil,* right next to the
São Carlos Opera House, where found objects are generally deposited.
Those found in public transport are deposited at the top of the Santa Justa
lift, off the Carmo Square.

Chambers of Commerce. *American Chamber of Commerce,* Rua Dona
Estefania 155 (tel. 572561); *British-Portuguese Chamber of Commerce,*
Rua Estrela 8 (tel. 661351).

Libraries. *American Library,* Ave. Duque de Loulé 22B (tel. 570102),
afternoons only; *British Institute,* Rua Luis Fernandes 3 (tel. 369208), with
library and reading room (closed for lunch, 12:30–2, and Wed. A.M.).

Bank. Lloyds Bank plc., Ave. da Liberdade 222 (tel. 535171) and Rua
do Ouro 40 (tel. 361211).

Churches. St. George's Church (Anglican), Rua São Jorge (tel. 663010), set in historical English cemetery; Corpo Santo Church (R.C.), Largo do Corpo Santo (tel. 323208), served by Irish Dominican Fathers; St. Andrew's Church of Scotland (Presbyterian), Rua Arriaga 13 (tel. 2844128).

THE ENVIRONS OF LISBON

Unlike the suburbs of many capital cities, those of Lisbon are attractive. However, there are still some shanty towns, particularly toward the airport.

The sea road out to Estoril and Cascais (N6) really starts after Belém, at Algés, with the great estuary of the Tagus to the left, and sandy beaches guarded by forts built to protect the sea approaches to Lisbon in the 17th century by King João IV, father of Catherine of Bragança who married King Charles II of England. This Estrada Marginal is bordered on the land side by private houses, many set in large gardens filled with brightly colored geraniums, bougainvilleas, bignonias, wisteria, cannas, roses and arum lilies, flowering in their different seasons, with the geraniums and bougainvilleas apparently in flower for most of the year. Constant electric trains also follow the sea from Cais do Sodré station in Lisbon to Cascais.

Estoril, Cascais and the Mouth of Hell

Inland, a four-lane motorway leads up from the Pombal statue at the top of the Avenida de Liberdade in Lisbon, through Monsanto Park until it joins the coast road between Cruz Quebrada and Caxias. The Estrada Marginal carries on through Paço d'Arcos, Oeiras, Carcavelos and Parede, which all have long, sandy beaches, to Cascais.

At Porto Salvo, behind Paço d'Arcos, there is an interesting museum which contains recently discovered terracotta urns and flat dishes of the era of the Emperor Diocletian. Nearby are freshly unearthed Roman ruins.

In Oeiras stands the small, 18th-century pink palace built by the Marquis of Pombal before he fell into disgrace. It is a delightful sight, with curved eaves to the pagoda-like roofs of the low, spreading buildings. In the grounds, now given over to horticultural research, are a charming Fishing Pavilion beside a great water tank backed by large blue and white azulejo panels, as well as other architectural features near the palace.

The town limits of Estoril are ill-defined and lost in greenery and building developments, but its center is the casino, where hopefuls throng the gaming tables and slot machines. The casino has a restaurant, cinema, exhibition space and a pretty winter garden. Wide avenues leading to the sea are lined with palm trees and first-rate hotels. This is a holiday world of suntan oil, of tennis-balls bouncing on well-kept courts.

Some of the beaches are hemmed in by low cliffs and submerged rocks. The best and longest beach is at Monte Estoril, which joins on to that of Estoril, where there are shops, snackbars, changing rooms, and beach chairs for hire. The houses climb the hill toward the golf course, their delightful shapes and colors half-hidden by the hibiscus bushes, the mimosa trees, the trailers of plumbago, as pale a blue as the sun-bleached sky. In late May and June the jacaranda trees are a mass of violet blue blossom, so thick that the new leaves are entirely hidden.

Within walking distance along the sea wall, and across the bay, lies Cascais, rival of Estoril. Between the two resorts rises the huge pile of the Hotel Estoril-Sol, 14 stories high, with its swimming pool, flowered terraces, and elegant shops.

Cascais is rich in history and tradition, and proud of her past. Here, the governor of the town was beheaded on the public square for opposing the forces of the Spanish Duke of Alba. Before the royal family went into exile in 1910 they came to Cascais with their court for the summer holidays, walking at ease through the town—then small—and greeting passers-by. A cove below the elegant Hotel Albatroz still bears the name of Queen's Beach.

For many years Cascais remained a fishing village, the boats being dragged up on to the sand, and the catch sold by Dutch auction nearby. Nowadays, the crates of newly caught fish are auctioned in a large covered space near the fishermen's beach, opposite the Hotel Baia.

In the 1930s, percipient painters and writers, some from overseas, rented the cottages above the rocky shore, worked when they felt like it, and drank endless cups of coffee in the cafés and endless glasses of wine in the taverns. But after World War II, more and more foreigners were attracted by the fishermen's houses, by the small squares filled with fishing nets hung out to dry in the sun, and the cobbled streets and steps leading down from the upper levels, so that now Cascais is filled with smart shops, particularly in the pedestrian Rua Frederico Arouca, with numerous restaurants and bars, plus a few hotels, residencias and pensions.

It was a fisherman of Cascais, according to local legend, who was first to discover America, ten years before Christopher Columbus. He was called Afonso Sanches, and during a voyage to the East Indies his boat was carried off to the coast of America. He managed to reach Madeira with two or three companions, exhausted like himself, who died soon after their arrival. Afonso Sanches was lodged by his friend, Columbus, a Genoese navigator, who had settled on the island after marrying the daughter of the Governor of Porto Santo. It was thanks to these men's ship's log that Columbus landed in the New World.

Marshal Carmona, President of the Republic for 22 years (1928–1950), whose favorite residence was, for a long time, the citadel, loved this time-worn shore, the old ramparts baked in the sun, and the people of the port, serious and industrious, who each day, no matter what the weather, put out to sea in their small boats to fish in open waters. On calm days you can see pork bladders painted bright red or yellow, and floated on the surface of the green water to indicate shoals of fish. Sometimes boats, in pairs, sails and masts lowered, rest side by side, connected by a great net, like those of the fishermen on the Lake of Tiberias.

The parish church of Cascais, at the top of the town, has some good paintings in it including a series by Josefa of Obidos and an elegant golden altar. Opposite the church is one of the entrances to delightful Castro Guimarães park, in which is a shallow lake with a café at one end, a small zoo, and tables and chairs set out under the trees for picknickers; to the west, on the road to Guincho, is the Museum. In a former private house bequeathed to the town by the owners, this museum has great charm, with beautiful objects alongside Edwardian splendor. At one end is a small archeological section with objects excavated from the neolithic tombs at Alapraia, near São João do Estoril. A library nearby has open shelves with quite a large English section, comfortable armchairs in which to read and, in the winter, a large fire burns in the hearth.

A greater attraction to travelers, the Boca do Inferno, or Mouth of Hell, is an awesome chasm in the rocks, where the inrushing sea is sucked down in a cream-colored whirlpool of water. Dozens of stalls selling local crafts line the road above. Soon the windswept coastline becomes rocky, and the cliffs crumble slowly into sea-wracked shingle.

The road passes a noble early 19th-century lighthouse, the Farol da Guia, and a number of small restaurants, each with its seawater tank occupied by swimming lobsters, crabs and crayfish for the future delectation of customers. To the right are two clubs, open to temporary members: the Dom Carlos has a fine swimming pool, tennis courts, riding facilities and a restaurant; the Quinta da Marinha has, in addition, a golf course designed by Robert Trent Jones.

After passing another, small 17th-century fortress on the low cliffs, a turning to the right, signposted Oitavos, leads up to the old semaphor station from which the arrival of ships was signaled before the invention of the telegraph. The building has been enlarged and is now a restaurant, from where you can look over a sea of umbrella pines to the Atlantic Ocean. Further west, as the trees fall back, dunes take over, and past another (later) lighthouse, at Cabo Raso, you come on to the superb Praia do Guincho. To the right is the long serrated line of the Sintra hills, dappled when the sun is shining, and to the left the grand profile of Cabo da Roca, the westernmost point of the continent of Europe. The beach is so long that the great rollers from the Atlantic pound unrelentingly on the sand even on calm days, so that swimming can be very dangerous. However, both wind- and boardsurfers find themselves in their element.

The strong pull of the tides throws up a wall of high waves which threaten to take the old fortress—now a superbly converted hotel—by storm, and to sweep the clapboard restaurants away to sea. People drive out from town to eat grilled lobster, stuffed crabs, and *percebes* (barnacles), which fill the mouth with the taste of the sea. The strong salt wind burns all that grows, save the hardy mesembryanthemum with pink and yellow flowers, whose fleshy leaves cover the autumn dunes with carpets of purple and rust. In late summer the sands above high tide are pierced with a lovely species of strongly scented white lily, *pancratium maritimum.*

The road (N247) then goes inland through a forest of pine and eucalyptus trees until Malveira da Serra, with its elegant houses, where it joins the road to Sintra (N9–1). Below the upward-winding road are amazing views of the Guincho and of the bare, stony country rolling away to the end of the Sintra range to your right. Several of the little villages above the sea are being gradually developed by people wanting to escape the trammels of town life. At the road's highest point, a left turning leads down to Cabo da Roca, passing through the village of Azoia with several good restaurants.

The Cape has an early lighthouse, built in 1772, which is surrounded by the now deserted but charming little houses of the lighthouse keepers who tended the great lamps before they were mechanized. There is plenty of parking space and even a small restaurant at this strange outpost, where the visitor feels the immensity of the ocean stretching away to the coast of the New World.

On the land side, a small building straddles the westernmost point of the Serra de Sintra. This is Peninha, in early times a hermitage when—as in so many early hermitages around the coasts of Europe—a light would presumably have burned at night to warn ships of the long headland below. The small chapel, even its ceiling, is entirely lined with blue and white tiled panels of New Testament scenes.

Monsanto Park

Some 50 years ago Lisbon was surrounded by thorny wastes, but in the intervening years the City Fathers have planted vast tracts of land with pine, eucalyptus and hardwoods, so that now Monsanto Park is a green thicket of trees, their scent blending with the sea breeze to freshen the air that blows through the city.

The vale of Alcantara is spanned by the lovely archways of the early 18th-century stone aqueduct, so solidly built that the earthquake of 1755 barely affected it. The central arches are enormously high, and the whole great ensemble is best seen from the motorway already mentioned, running from the Pombal statue to the coast. After this the highway speeds on between the trees, mingled with mimosa or yellow gorse, heather or rose laurel, according to the time of year.

If you have time, drive off the highway and up a road to the Alto da Serafina, where you will be rewarded by a bird's-eye view of the city and the river. From the heights of Serafina you will have a night view of an enchanted city, streets and river and bridge twinkling with lights, beneath the statue of Christ the King.

Lisbon's camping ground here, with its green spaces, shady trees, big swimming pool, post office, shops, hairdresser, laundry and cafeteria, is a model of its kind.

Queluz

The most attractive of the royal residences is the Rococo palace of Queluz on the way to Sintra (N17). The estate has always been the endowment of the royal princes, or rather, the younger sons of the king. It was there that, in 1667, Pedro, second living son of João IV, went into retirement, to plan the bold move that was to give him both the throne and the wife of his older brother, Afonso VI.

In 1758, the future Pedro III entrusted two architects, the Portuguese Mateus Vicente de Oliveira and the Frenchman Jean Baptiste Robillon, with the construction of his miniature Versailles in place of the house he had inherited. Finished in 1794, the elegant pink palace turns its best front to the formal gardens, where statues and azulejos frame pools and fountains. A stately Throne Room and graceful Music Room, decked out with fresco scrolls and flower garlands, painted ceilings and gilt mirrors, enclose elegant 18th-century furniture. One room, lined with chinoiserie tiles, has charming bamboo armchairs.

Pedro IV was born and died in Don Quixote's Room, but Queluz was put at times to more sinister use than chamber music concerts by candlelight and courtly gatherings in the gilded ballroom. Plots against Pombal were whispered in its corners; and Queen Carlota Joaquina, Spanish wife of João VI, banished from Lisbon, here held her opposition court. Outside there are a few strange touches: the stone sphinxes with ruffs and ribbons above their women's breasts, looking blindly down the leafy alleys; the great theatrical stairway over the cages, behind whose bars the wild beasts once paced imprisoned; the slow stream down which boats drifted to the sound of music between the walls of azulejos, while men and girls played a sophisticated hide and seek in the boxwood maze, long since destroyed.

Queen Elizabeth II of Great Britain stayed in the charming Pavilion of Queen Maria, residence of visiting heads of state. Other parts still in use are the chapel, often the scene of smart weddings, and Cozinha Velha, the old palace kitchen, now a luxurious restaurant and tearoom serving the old royal recipes. The palace is closed on Tuesdays.

Not far from Queluz, at São Domingos de Benfica, the Fronteira Palace stands in superb formal gardens with statuary and a long water tank backed by iridescent tiles of heroic-sized prancing horsemen, each different. Visitors can wander in the lovely demesne and visit the palace (see *Places of Interest* at end of this chapter).

Sintra and its Palaces

Whereas in Estoril and on the Sun Coast the sea breeze blows the clouds away from a clear sky, even in winter, the hills or *serra* of Sintra gather the sea mists and, even in summer, stay fresh and cool. No sun can dry the water that wells up from the rich earth, patched blue with periwinkles. When the heat snaps the pine twigs and bursts open the sweet-smelling eucalyptus buds, the walls stay green with moss along the road that winds from Pena Palace to Colares through the silent forest of Sintra. The diminutive cells of the abandoned monastery of Capuchos are lined with cork to keep out the damp.

The road passes by some of the finest country houses in Portugal, belonging to the classes privileged by birth or money, talent or taste. They house collections of old weapons or china, ivories or music scores, and in the gardens there are stone basins shaded by lemon trees, tree ferns, roses and wild lavender.

A few live in Sintra the year round, most in summer only. Some have noble houses, with a private chapel and stables. Others have simple dwellings, taking pride in a giant magnolia or a magnificent view. All are under the spell of Sintra, from which there is no release.

Like all enchanted places, Sintra can disappoint the newcomer. Never go there in low spirits, or in bad weather. The local saying goes that if the Sintra hills are hidden by cloud, or if the donkeys are braying, better stay away.

The lovers of Sintra take pleasure in this white weather, when mists catch and tear on the spurs of rock and the tops of tall trees, when the glazed tiles sweat with water, and wisps of cloud drift soundlessly through the broken ramparts of the old Moorish castle. At times, the fog is so dense that the peak-top Palace of Pena disappears from view. Cars move slowly, in a yellow blur of headlights. Frogs splash in the stone basins, among the floating camellia petals. Distance is within touch, the world is small and cold, and you feel the need of a fireside and hot tea. Meanwhile, the hapless traveler, walled in by the white silence, is lost in the unknown.

A shift in the wind will all at once blow the mists away, revealing the stone cross on the hilltop, bringing back sight and sound. Lizards dart through the undergrowth, the air smells strongly of moss, wet bark, and magnolias. The roof of the Pena shines in the sun, the light falls bright on the tangle of greenery. Horse-drawn carriages trot slowly up the steep and winding ways that lead to the monastery of the Capuchos or to the Cruz Alta, and fireflies flit through the warm evening air in May.

The Castelo dos Mouros

The castle of the Moors dates back to the 7th century. Its stone walls rise from a natural rampart of rocks, making it safe from enemy attack. The sentry path has a sweeping view over the plain and down to the sea. The fortress was safeguarded against all dangers, whether enemy soldiers, thirst, or hunger, by lookouts, deep cisterns, and underground vaults. And yet it fell, as did the castles in Lisbon and Palmela, taken by storm by Afonso Henriques and his men-at-arms in 1147.

Abandoned, the old Moorish castle is overrun by brambles; the stone steps crumble underfoot, birds nest in the battlements, and on wintry days the wind sighs through the empty cisterns. It is a wild, still place, a haunt of loneliness, unrelieved in its gloom.

The Paço da Vila

If the Arabs had built a fortress on the hilltop, it was to keep watch over the valley, but the Palace was built far below, in a bower of cypress and palm trees.

Most of the kings of Portugal have loved Sintra, and left their mark on her. What Windsor is to the history of England, St. Germain-en-Laye to the history of France, the Paço da Vila in Sintra is to the history of Portugal.

Dinis, the poet king, of whom an old song tells that "he did all that he pleased," resided in this palace. But it was the Aviz dynasty that built the Paço da Vila and King John I planned here the expedition to Ceuta in 1415, and it was also here that he betrothed his daughter Isabela to the powerful Philip of Burgundy. To bring back his bride, the duke had sent a token court of chosen envoys, among whom was the renowned painter Van Eyck, whose style so strongly influenced Nuno Gonçalves. In memory of the wedding, the king ordered a ceiling in the palace to be painted with swans, emblem both of the princess and of her husband's capital city, Bruges. This is a particularly lovely and unusual room, long and narrow, with splendid Chinese porcelain bird tureens on the tables. State banquets sometimes take place here.

In Sintra, too, King João was caught kissing a lady-in-waiting of his English queen, Philippa of Lancaster, daughter of John of Gaunt, one of England's great warriors. The king swore that the kiss was *por bem,* without consequence, and his wife believed him; but the incident gave rise to such gossip that the king, exasperated, ordered a ceiling in the palace to be painted with as many magpies as there were chattering court ladies. Each bird is different and has in its claw the red rose of Lancaster, and, by its beak, the words: POR BEM, to cry the king's blamelessness throughout the ages.

Perhaps, on taking her husband's word, Queen Philippa was thinking of her grandfather, King Edward III of England, who, also married to a Philippa, and caught with a lady's garter in his hand, created the Order of the Garter, bearing the words HONI SOIT QUI MAL Y PENSE: Shame be to him who evil thinks.

Afonso V, nicknamed the African, seldom lived within his kingdom; but he was born and died in Sintra, in the same bed-chamber.

It was to Manuel I, however, that the Paço owed its crowning glory. The Fortunate King, as he was known, undertook to enlarge and embellish the old palace in a Moorish style that is not, as is often supposed, the work of its Arab builders, but the result of a taste brought back from Manuel's travels in Spain, where he had seen and admired the horseshoe windows, the multicolored azulejos, and the flowered patios murmuring with water. It is to his love of Andalusian artistry that we owe the tall chimneys, the sunlit fountains in the orange-scented courtyards, and the ceiling painted with the coats-of-arms of the noble families in his kingdom. In this hall, he received with royal pomp ambassadors and poets, among them Gil Vicente. Here, too, he held his courts of love, gave banquets, and watched his Moorish dancing girls.

In the sunset of a dying dynasty, sitting on the bench of glazed tiles in the Patio of the Negress, young King Sebastião listened to Camões reading his *Lusiad.* Fired by the epic of his forebears' glory, the foolhardy boy led an army to conquer Morocco, but was doomed to total defeat and death.

Sintra was to be a prison for a yet more unfortunate king. Afonso VI, bereft of his throne and his wife by his ambitious younger brother, betrayed, half mad, lived the nine years until his death locked up in a palace room, wearing out the flagstones with his ceaseless pacing.

The earthquake of 1755 shook the old walls, cracked the tiles, split the painted wood and crumbled the plaster arabesques. However, while the royal residences in Lisbon, in Evora, in Santarém and in Almeirim were destroyed or damaged beyond repair, the old Paço in Sintra stood steadfast, surviving both the havoc of nature and clumsy restoration.

There are the kitchens, with vast conical chimneys in Moorish style, the great echoing rooms with their polished floors, their decorated ceilings: the Swan Room, the Mermaids' Room, and the Escutcheon Room. Near the palace windows, seats of azulejos remind one of countless queens and princesses who must have sat there with their embroidery, waiting for their husbands to come back from hunting expeditions or the wars. There are even Edwardian rooms, to the right of the entrance hall, charmingly decorated for King Carlos, who was assassinated in 1908, and his wife Queen Amélia. If the guide does not take you in to these elegant rooms, ask him to do so as they are worth seeing for the price of a tip.

The Palácio da Pena

The 19th century did not find the old Paço to its taste. Queen Maria's second husband, Ferdinand of Coburg, anticipated the building mania of his mad relative, Ludwig of Bavaria. In 1840 he began to transform the monastery built by Manuel I between 1503 and 1511 on the topmost hill of Sintra into a pseudo-medieval palace, a sample patchwork of every style of architecture, with Arab minarets and Gothic turrets, Renaissance cupolas and gazebos, together with a few fantasies of his own. The resulting jumble is something of a curiosity, saved by the natural beauty of its setting. The gardens and rocky woods and its height above the surrounding countryside all combine to give a strange feeling of unreality.

The years have passed. The Portuguese kings are dead. The Pena's ill-matched styles, all equally bygone, are bound together by time. Indoors, the Victorian furnishings—deer antlers, Saxe porcelains, plush chairs and antimacassars—unfashionable for so long, have now come back into favor.

At a lower level lies a botanical park, in which nothing is missing: stone ponds with gliding swans; fountains with different tasting waters, all spring-cold and refreshing; clusters of camellias, streams and Japanese bridges, rock gardens, summer houses and grottos; even a gigantic stone man in armor, among the umbrella pines. (Baron Von Eschweg, the architect of Pena.) There are hothouses, tree ferns, dwarf cedars, gulches, and a barren stretch of under-brush, over which the sparrow-hawks wheel unceasingly. For a slight extra charge automobiles or taxis can drive through the narrow winding roads of this great estate. The Palácio da Vila is closed on Wednesdays, the Pena on Mondays.

Sintra

If, being a tourist, you cannot hope for an invitation to one of the wonderful *quintas,* or country houses, in Sintra, you can always offer yourself the luxury of going to the palace of Seteais, now a hotel.

At the end of the 18th century it was built by a Dutch consul who made a fortune in Brazilian diamonds, and who there received, in great style, King João VI and his queen. To honor the event, he built a second identical wing to his house, joining it to the first by an arch of triumph which frames the overhanging Palácio da Pena on one side, and on the other the valley of Colares. On an outcropping of rock in the garden, Byron sat to write enthusiastically about Sintra in the shade of laurel leaves, as befits a poet.

Today, the house, still in harmony with an age of elegance and leisure, stays renowned for its good fare as a luxury hotel, set in lawns, boxwood and roses, the evening air scented with sun-warmed heliotrope. The hotel's name comes from *sete ais,* seven sighs—of relief by the Portuguese, after the signing of the Treaty of Sintra in 1807, by which Junot pledged himself and his French troops to leave Portugal, though they were back again in 1808!

The 18th-century Palace of Ramalhão, on the direct road between Estoril and Sintra, has lovely wall-paintings; once a royal palace, it is now a school and convent, and not open to the public. Also regrettably closed to the public are the 16th-century Palace of Ribafrias and the neo-Manueline Manor of Regaleira—an extraordinary example of late-Victorian fantasy just before Seteais. More accessible are the Library-Museum with its pictures and prints in the Palace of Valenças, the Gothic Churches of Santa Maria and São Pedro, the latter with great tiled panels, the Church of São Martinho in the town, and the circular chapel at Janas, towards the sea, scene of a big *romaria* and fair on August 17, when people bring their animals to be blessed.

In São Pedro de Sintra, a fair is held on the second and fourth Sundays of each month. Livestock is sold, and harness and seeds and boots, together with flowers, fruit, and vegetables. But you will also find old prints, pewter tankards, glass, fob watches and gilt wood, all jumbled together with rusty lanterns and artless earthenware pottery, beside an old woman in a black shawl selling *queijadas,* the sweet cheese tartlets that are a specialty in Sintra.

A very strange property, Monserrate, on the way to Colares, was built at the whim of a rich Englishman, Sir Francis Cook, an early 19th-century merchant from the City of London. A Turkish harem in marble, Etruscan tombs, a fretwork chalet, form an incongruous yet impressive whole. But the beauty of Monserrate lies in its gardens, laid out at a time when travel was long and difficult; the seedlings that survived the journey were planted outdoors in alien weather, to take root and grow beside the simple plane tree and the hardy palm. There you will find the greatest variety of ferns in the world, together with giant daturas, strawberry trees, bamboos, and plants that have elsewhere lost popularity long ago, like the Chinese gingko and the monkey puzzle.

On the road running north from Sintra to Ericeira lies Odrinhas. The Archeological Museum of São Miguel de Odrinhas here is of great interest, containing pieces from the first century B.C. In the well-kept garden surrounding the museum are traces of a Paleo-Christian temple and some lovely mosaics.

Colares and the Sea

Colares is a region of countryfolk and vine-growers, of good wine to be drunk with hearty food at tables under the trees, overlooking a stone bridge and a slow-flowing stream half choked with grasses and wild flowers. The village of Colares, up the hill, is still unspoilt with charming color-washed houses and cottages. The road goes on up to Penedo, another delightful group of pretty houses.

Between Colares and the sea, the road is lined with holiday homes, partly hidden by the pinewoods of Banzão. The pines go down to the sands of Praia das Maçãs, a beach with a swimming pool and camping ground.

Nearby is Praia Grande, a yet longer sandy beach with thundering breakers.

Farther still, the coastline grows wilder, the cliffs pitted with mussel-studded coves. A mile or so away lies Azenhas do Mar, a white village on a high ledge of rock. Far below, the tide-mills that gave the place its name have become swimming pools, washed by the waves of the incoming sea.

The woods and pastures on either side of the road abound in wild flowers in early spring, before the torrid sun has dried the soil to a hard red crust on which only cistus, heather and low heaths can survive the long summer months.

The farther you go, the wilder the seascape; until you see, jutting forward like the prow of a ship, the headland of Cabo da Roca, Europe's westernmost point, where the Serra of Sintra drops to the sea.

The Northern Suburbs

At the other end of the Campo Grande is Lumiar, a once delightful village now dominated by the motorways cutting through it. Lumiar has two entertaining museums: a Costume Museum set in the lovely gardens of the Duke of Palmela's *Quinta,* with a good, expensive restaurant, and a Theater Museum in the equally lovely Palace of Monteiro Mor next door.

You can catch a glimpse beyond of a curious fountain whose colored tiles tell—somewhat like cartoon-strips—how the Odivelas church was desecrated in 1671 by a thief, and how he was subsequently punished. Now submerged into the almost nameless city suburbs, the history of Odivelas is a long one. King Dinis asked to be buried here under the fine old trees in the square together with his royal spouse, Isabel, the "Beggar Queen." But later the Saint-Queen's body was moved to Coimbra, the whole church being perfumed with the scent of roses when her remains were transferred to a solid silver tomb. Here, too, in 1415, Queen Philippa died of the plague, after solemnly bestowing on her sons, who were on their way to Ceuta, the swords emblematic of their knighthood.

In the 18th century, the convent resembled a finishing school for well-born young ladies, renowned for their soirées of poetry readings and receptions with music, with which the nuns entertained callers. A goodly number of these charming girls did not lack for romantic adventure: the best-known story that has come down to us concerns the long and passionate romance of King João V and Madre Paula.

At Loures is the fine country house of Correio Mor built by a Postmaster General in the late 18th century. A road leads due west out of Loures, through Caneças and past the headwaters of the Lisbon aqueduct, with its splendid stone conduits and small water towers, striding off across a still largely deserted countryside to Queluz.

South of the Tagus

The bridge over the Tagus opens the road to the south, but no pedestrians are allowed on it. However, one can still cross the river from Caes de Sodré and Praça do Comércio by ferry boat, which docks in Cacilhas (the former ferry takes cars). Cacilhas is backed by the low-price suburb of Almada, where tall buildings are fast reaching out towards the Costa da Caparica. The 34 km. (21 miles) of fine sand can be dangerous for the unwary swimmer, as is the equally exposed coast beyond Sintra, where huge breakers often close the beaches. Several new resorts near Caparica are just on the verge of becoming popular but in the lonely sand dunes of the southern end you may still escape from the world.

The motorway to the south is lined with pinewoods, studded with summer cottages and drive-in restaurants; and even though there are many signs of growing industrial involvement and spreading suburban sprawl, there are still also long unspoiled stretches of trees and rice paddies, silent under the sun but for the strong beating of wings as the storks swoop down on the croaking frogs.

A village at a crossroads on the old highway, Azeitão is well worth a stopover. There is a remarkable fountain in carved stone, an old church, and fine old houses. The shops sell a good muscatel wine and a renowned ewes' milk cheese.

Along the road to Setúbal, a strange science-fiction area of white domes visible on the left is in fact a modern winery which produces a delicious wine, famous for centuries, under up-to-the-minute conditions. Visitors are welcome. Another fine old dwelling, the Quinta das Torres, is now a guesthouse and restaurant. Overlooking a large ornamental water tank with a miniature temple rising from the waters and a leafy park, the rooms are full of antique furniture and paintings, polished brass and firearms, sunlight and green shadows. In winter, it is alight with the glow and scent of woodfires.

Bacalhoa, one of the earliest inhabited houses in the country, is a beautiful late 16th-century L-shaped building, its corners adorned with canteloupe-melon cupolas. Arched terraces overlook the box-hedged gardens, and the air is filled with the heady scent of orange trees. The great water tank washes a pavilion with pyramidal towers which houses the earliest dated tile panel in the country, that of Susannah and the Elders, 1565. The house, with full staff, can now be rented by the week.

Fork left for Palmela, with a huge Templar's Castle crowning the hilltop above a network of cobbled streets between low white-washed houses. The Castle, with a luxury pousada installed in the 18th-century buildings at one end, is fascinating, with superb views towards Lisbon and the "Sea of Straw," bathed in a filmy light. To the south lies Setúbal and the river Sado with its still waters and rice paddies beyond groves of the orange trees for which the district is famous.

Branching to the right, in Azeitão, the road leads to Sesimbra, now surrounded by high-rise apartment houses, but by the sea and still a lively fishing village where many Lisboans have a summer house. Perched on a hilltop, the five towers of an old castle overlook the port on the rounded beach, guarded by a fortress, and littered with boats, coils of rope, and anchors.

Traveling west along the excellent road, you will be rewarded by the view from Cape Espichel, a salt-encrusted headland on which 18th-century arcaded pilgrim houses border a huge open space. At one end is a great forsaken pilgrimage church in this lonely land's end given over to silence and seagulls. Behind the church the turf above the low cliffs is alive with wild flowers in the spring, though the scene is somewhat marred by strange modernistic sculptures placed at random and looking very much out of place in this calm 18th-century atmosphere. To the north, unsullied beaches extend up to Caparica, for no roads lead to these remote sands which take the full force of the Atlantic gales. Big romarias are held here on August 15 and on the last Sunday in September.

The Serra d'Arrábida

It is loneliness and silence, and the boundless seascape, that the monks were seeking in the barren range of Arrábida, where they built a monastery on a southern slope of the hills. A striking statue by Frei Martinho greets the traveler: arms outstretched in a cross stands a monk with heart and mouth shut by a padlock. The white walls of the monastery cling to the hillside, falling away into the brilliant sea.

The hills are covered by a scratchy underbrush of thorn bushes, stunted lentisk and juniper trees, gnarled oaks and prickly pears, survivors of the primeval forest of the peninsula; here and there, the green distaff of a cypress tree springs skywards from the stony ground that crumbles down to the sheltered beach of Portinho d'Arrábida, lying like a shell among the jutting rocks. The old fortress has been turned into an Estalagem, where outdoor tables under a vine trellis look over and down into the glass-clear water. On summer Sundays, Mass is said in the grotto of Santa Margarida, visited by Hans Christian Andersen when he was in Portugal in 1866. Far away, the sun shines on the sands of Troia, the long peninsula at the mouth of the river Sado, which is now becoming a popular resort.

Two roads along the hills lead to the old, but industrialized, town of Setúbal, at the foot of the Castelo de São Filipe, inside the walls of which there is a pousada. The sheltered harbor, the nearby stretches of salt-pans, the plentiful catch of sardines, have given rise to a rich canning industry. The town is also renowned for red mullet, and muscatel wine, the last in great favor at the table of Louis XIV. It prides itself on being the birthplace of the poet Bocage, and on the fine Manueline church of Jesus, with strange twisted columns and handsome porch of Arrábida marble.

Alongside is the Municipal Museum, containing a series of lovely Portuguese paintings in Baroque frames which were taken out of the Church of Jesus some years ago.

Ferry boats taking cars connect Setúbal with the beautiful beach of Troia and the sunken ruins of the old Roman city of Cetóbriga, engulfed in the year 412. Large-scale development is taking place, and the whole atmosphere of the area is rapidly changing.

An 18-hole par 72 golf course designed by Robert Trent Jones stretches alongside the River Sado at Troia, with natural water hazards cleverly incorporated in some of the fairways. Tennis courts are also available, at a reasonable price.

PRACTICAL INFORMATION FOR
THE ENVIRONS OF LISBON

TOURIST OFFICES. There are local tourist offices in the following towns: **Almada,** Rua Conde Ferreira 8; **Cabo da Roca,** Cabo da Roca; **Cas-**

cais, Ave. D. Carlos 1; **Costa da Caparica,** Praça da Liberdade; **Ericeira,** Rua Eduardo Burnay 33A; **Estoril,** Arcadas do Parque; **Palmela,** Largo do Chafariz; **Sesimbra,** Ave. dos Naufragios; **Setúbal,** Rua do Corpo Santo; **Sintra,** Praça da Republica.

HOTELS AND RESTAURANTS

Alcabideche (Lisbon), on the road from Estoril to Sintra. *Sintra Estoril* (M), tel. 2690720. 187 rooms with bath. Indoor pool, tennis, sauna, garage, 9-hole golf course and autodrome nearby. AE, DC, MC, V.

Azeitão (Setúbal), south of Lisbon. *Estalagem Quinta das Torres* (I), tel. 2080001. 10 rooms with bath. Former private residence with charming old-world atmosphere and set in real country, ideal for walkers. Good food; in summer, dine in the garden by the pool, or indoors by candlelight. Two independent cottages in grounds.

Bacalhoa. Superb 16th-century country house. 5 double, 2 single rooms with bath. Full staff. Pool. Minimum booking one week for up to 8 people. Apply, Thomas Scoville, 3637 Veazey St. N.W., Washington DC, 20008.

Bucelas. Home of the wine drunk by Wellington's officers.
Restaurants. *Barrete Saloio* (I), (tel. 9854004). Good home cooking. Closed Tues. *Casarão* (I), (tel. 9854511). Closed Mon.

Cacilhas (Setúbal). **Restaurants.** Several restaurants on river wall, with price lists displayed outside. Get a table by the window and see the lights of Lisbon come up over the Tagus as you eat, or watch the porpoises playing, in rough weather.

Carcavelos (Lisbon). *Praia Mar* (M), tel. 2473131. 158 rooms with bath. Modern hotel with sea view and pool, shops; almost on the beach. **Restaurants.** There are several beach restaurants.

Cascais (Lisbon), a short train ride from Lisbon. *Albatroz* (E), Rua Frederico Arouca 100 (tel. 282921). 40 rooms with bath. On low rocks above the sea, an attractive old house, now extended and modernized, but retaining its character. Charming bedrooms, dining room with picture windows looking on to the sea, terrace bar, pool, garage. Especially good for summer. Recommended. AE, DC, MC, V. *Cidadela* (E), Ave. 25 de Abril (tel. 282921). 115 rooms with bath, plus 15 self-contained apartments overlooking garden and swimming pool, shops, garage, restaurant. Pleasant but noisy. AE, DC, MC, V. *Estalagem da Guia* (E), Estrada do Guincho (tel. 289239). 29 rooms with bath. Pool. AE, DC, MC, V. *Estoril Sol* (E), on the Estrada Marginal (tel. 282831). 310 rooms with bath and balcony. Restaurant and bar on 9th floor with panoramic view; warm seawater pool, sauna, Health Club Soleil, disco, shops, garage. AE, DC, MC, V.
Baia (M), Ave. Marginal (tel. 281033). 85 rooms with bath. Noisy, but lovely view over Fishermen's Beach. Handy restaurant terrace. AE, DC, MC, V. *Nau* (M), Rua Dra. Iracy Doyle 2 (tel. 282861). 54 rooms with bath. AE, DC, MC, V. *Nossa Senhora das Preces* (M), Rua Visconde de Gandarinha 43

(tel. 280376). 15 rooms with bath. Secluded country house in wooded outskirts; pool, tennis; restaurant with good local cooking. AE, DC, MC, V.

Equador (I), Alto da Pampilheira (tel. 2840524). 117 service apartments with bath and kitchenette. Pool, sauna, supermarket, etc. Very good value; not in center. AE, DC, MC. *Valbom* (I), Ave. Valbom 14 (tel. 2865801). 40 rooms with bath. Simple and a bit basic; breakfast only; garage. In heart of town. AE, DC, MC, V.

Restaurants. *Adega do Morgado* (E), Ave. Marechal Carmona 1 (tel. 2867198). Country decor; parking. Closed Mon. in winter. AE, DC, MC. *Baluarte* (E), Ave. D. Carlos 1 (tel. 2865471). Picture windows overlooking the bay. Always open. AE, DC, MC. *Batel* (E), Travessa das Flores (tel. 280215). Excellent seafood, prompt service, quiet decor. Always open. AE, DC, MC. *Dom Leitão* (E), Ave. Vasco da Gama 36 (tel. 2865487). Roast sucking pig; a specialty—but a distinctly tourist-orientated place, with occasionally cavalier service. Closed Wed. AE, DC, MC. *João Padeiro* (E), Rua Visconde da Luz 12 (tel. 280232). Best sole on the coast, served in atmospheric decor (ancient leather-lined walls). Closed Sun. dinner. AE, DC, MC. *John Bull* (E), Praça Costa Pinto 31 (tel. 283319). On main street, with fireplace, easy chairs, prints on the wall—small and crowded restaurant with pub downstairs. Always open. AE, DC, MC. *Pescador* (E), Rua das Flores 10 (tel. 282054). Good seafood. Very folksy with low, cluttered ceiling. Always open. AE, DC, MC. *Pimentão* (E), Rua das Flores 16 (tel. 2840994). Comfortable, stylish place with good food and attractive downstairs bar. Always open. AE, DC, MC. *Reijos* (E), Rua Frederico Arouca 35 (tel. 280311). Small, American-owned and with real hamburgers. Always open. *Visconde da Luz* (E), Jardim Visconde da Luz (tel. 2866848). Good food and obliging staff; don't be put off by woodland exterior. Closed Tues. AE, DC, MC.

Alho Porro (M), Rua Alexandre Herculano 13 (tel. 2868660). Excellent fish and grills. Closed Mon. AE, DC, MC. *Burladero* (M), Praça dos Touros (tel. 2868751). Recommended. Closed Tues., also Wed. lunch. AE, DC, MC. *O Caixote* (M), Rua Carlos Ribeiro 3 (tel. 2845001). Friendly place, Austrian-run. Happy hour from 6–7 in the evening. Special tourist menu. Very near station. *Frango Real* (M), Ave. 25 de Abril 17C (tel. 2868186). Specializes in chicken. Closed Wed. AE, DC, MC. *Gil Vicente* (M), Rua dos Novagantes 22 (tel. 282032). Excellent cooking. AE, DC, MC, V.

Casa do Largo (I). Very attractively designed bar close to the fort (just along from the Ceramica). Simple food, and pleasant clientele. *Castro* (I), Rua das Flores 12 (tel. 280901). Fresh seafood and a friendly atmosphere. Located behind the fish market. Closed Thurs. *Duke of Wellington Bar* (I), Rua Frederico Arouca 32 (tel. 280394). Busy bar, canned music, cheerful atmosphere and indifferent food. Always open. *Pigalo* (I), Travessa Frederico Arouca 12 (tel. 282802). Small, intimate, very good value; near station. Closed Wed. *Santini* (I), Ave. Valbom 28F (tel. 283709). For the best ices on the coast. Open summer only; closed Mon. *Victor* (I), Rua Visconde da Luz 43A (tel. 282344). Closed Mon. Very good value.

Nightlife. *Forte Dom Rodrigo,* Casa Santa Isabel, Estrada de Birre (tel. 2851373). The smartest place to hear fados. *Kopus Bar,* Largo das Grutas 3 (tel. 2845201). For fados. Open daily 9 P.M.–3 A.M. *Van Gogo,* Travessa Alfarrobeira 9 (tel. 283378). Dancing. Open daily 11 P.M.–4 A.M. AE, DC, MC.

Caxias. Restaurants. *Monaco* (E), Estrada Marginal (tel. 2432339). Picture windows on to sea; dancing, live music; parking. AE, DC, MC, V. *Trigal* (I), Mercado 7–8 (tel. 2433249). Good local food and wine.

Colares (Lisbon). *Estalagem do Conde* (I), Quinta do Conde (tel. 9291652). 11 rooms with bath. An interesting find: beautiful views, several orchard-set cottages. Pleasant but remote (car essential). DC, MC. *Miramonte* (I), Pinhal da Nazaré, Banzão (tel. 9291230). 72 rooms with bath. English-owned; good value; garden. On road to Praia das Maças.

Costa Da Caparica (Setúbal). Across the river from Lisbon and only a short drive by bus from Cacilhas, 34 km. (21 miles) of long sandy beach beloved by Lisboans, many of whom own small cottages along the beach. Much frequented by painters and writers. A small train takes you along the dunes if you don't want to walk. There are many small pensions. *Estalagem Colibri* (M), Ave. 1 de Maio (tel. 2900573). 25 rooms with bath. *Praia do Sol* (I), Rua dos Pescadores 12 (tel. 2900012). 54 rooms with bath. Breakfast only. AE, DC, MC.

Restaurants. Several small restaurants, mostly (I). *Carolina do Aires* (M), Ave. General Humberto Delgado (tel. 2900124). Parking. AE, DC, MC.

Estoril (Lisbon). A short electric train-ride from Lisbon. (See also Monte Estoril.) Casino. There are several pensions. *Palácio* (L), Casino Gardens (tel. 2680400). 200 rooms and suites with bath. Front rooms have nice view; park, heated pool, Health Club Soleil; good food. Considered the most elegant. AE, DC, MC, V.

Anka (E), Estrada Marginal (tel. 2681811). 89 rooms with bath. Magnificent view over bay; seascape from the top-floor terrace-restaurant is picturesque by day and bewitching by night. AE, DC, MC, V. *Lennox Country Club* (E), Rua Eng. Alv. P. Sousa 5 (tel. 2680424). 32 rooms with bath. Very comfortable; a favorite with golfers, who can have all-in terms including golf and transport to the course. Small pool; good food. Garage. AE, DC, MC, V.

Lido (M), Rua Alentejo 12 (tel. 2684098). 62 rooms with bath. In quiet street, not close to the beach. Pool; good food and good value. AE, DC, MC, V.

Apartementos Alvorada (I), tel. 2680070. 51 rooms with bath. Pleasant and good value; breakfast only; facing Casino. AE, DC, MC. *Estalagem Belvedere* (I), Rua Dr. António Martins 8 (tel. 2689163). 16 rooms with bath. Excellent food. AE, DC, MC. *Estalagem do Fundador* (I), Ave. D. Alfonso Henriques 11 (tel. 2682221). 12 rooms. Friendly bar; mainly English-speaking guests. *Estalagem Pica Pau* (I), Ave. D. Alfonso Henriques 48 (tel. 2680556). 48 rooms with bath. AE, DC, MC. *Inglaterra* (I), Rua do Porto (tel. 2684461). 49 rooms with bath. Good family hotel, with pool. Breakfast only. *Paris* (I), Estrada Marginal (tel. 2680018). 78 rooms with bath. Pool, disco. Rather noisy. AE, DC, MC, V.

Restaurants. *Casino* (E), (tel. 2680176). Dinner with floor show; dancing. You will need your passport to get into the gaming rooms. AE, DC, MC, V. *Choupana* (E), Estrada Marginal (tel. 2683099). Right on the sea on the approach to Estoril. The smartest place along the coast, and the food is rightly famous: the bill is high, but you get what you want plus the view. Band, dancing, parking. Always open. AE, DC, MC, V. *Four Seasons* (E), in

Hotel Palácio, Casino Gardens (tel. 2680400). Parking. Closed for lunch out of season. AE, DC, MC, V. *Frolic* (E), Ave. Clothilde (tel. 2681219). Under the Palácio, you dine well in gilded splendor; spacious dance floor; enjoyable bar. Always open. AE, DC, MC, V. *Furusato,* Praia do Tamariz (tel. 2683512). Luxurious decor, good Japanese food. Expensive.

Deck Bar (M), Arcadas do Parque (tel. 2680366). Under the arcades near the Tourist Bureau. Noisy, never a dull moment. Closed Mon. *Garrett* (M), Ave. Nice (tel. 2680365). Tearoom just past the Post Office going up Avenida Nice, serving lunches *à la carte,* on covered terrace or inside. Quiet and restful. Closed Tues. *Golf Club* (M), Ave. da Republica (tel. 2680176). Restaurant open to public. Lunch only. DC, MC. *Pickwick Club* (M), Ave. Biarritz 3G (tel. 2686726). AE, DC, MC. *Tamariz* (M), tel. 2683512. Snackbar on the beach. Open in summer only. AE, DC, MC.

Curry House (I), Ave. Marginal 60 (tel. 2680393). Delicious Goan food. Friendly service. Also has 14 good rooms with breakfast. Parking.

Guincho (Lisbon). A beautiful stretch of sandy beach (beware the heavy undertow) beyond Cascais. A car is essential if you stay, although there are buses in and out of Cascais. For a quiet sun-and-sea rest with really good food and comfortable rooms you can hardly do better than to take en pension terms at one of the hotels listed below.

Hotel do Guincho (E), tel. 2850491. 36 rooms with bath. One of the most attractive hotels in Portugal—an old fort converted with superb craftsmanship; on the beach. A romantic setting, whether for a stay, dinner or just for drinks. Topnotch restaurant with excellent service. Guest can use the pool at the *Estoril-Sol* hotel, Cascais. Check availability, as seems to be closed often without warning. AE, DC, MC, V. *Quinta da Marinha* (E), tel. 289881. 40 self-service villas. Restaurant, pool, 18-hole golf course, tennis, riding.

Estalagem do Forte Muchaxo (M), tel. 2850221. 24 rooms with bath. Seawater pool. Started life as a simple hut where fishermen could buy drinks and coffee; the hut remains but the estalagem is an attractive building on the beach with splendid views from the rooms—price depends on the view! If you don't come for a room, certainly come for the food, especially the seafood. AE, DC, MC, V.

Estalagem Mar do Guincho (I), tel. 2850251. 13 rooms with bath. Also known by its original restaurant name of *Mestre Zé;* pleasant rooms with a stunning view. Shellfish a specialty, but expensive; other seafoods more moderate. AE, DC, MC.

Restaurants. As might be expected, the restaurants in the area are particularly good for seafood. To find a restaurant overlooking the entire coast, drive along the Cascais–Guincho road, look for the sign to Oitavos, and there drive up the short steep road to the old semaphore station. *Abano* (E), tel. 2850221. On the cliffs above an enchanting tiny beach at Praia do Abano, reached over a bumpy road signposted on the left about 200 meters along the road from Guincho towards Malveira da Serra. Closed Tues. AE, DC, MC. *Faroleiro* (E), tel. 2850225. The first restaurant to be opened in the Guincho, located on the far side of the road out of sight of the sea, but the food is very good and, of course, lobster is always available, at a price, prepared in several ways. Always open. AE, DC, MC. *Furnas Lagosteiras* (E), Estrada do Guincho (tel. 289243). One of several right on the sea. There are a few tables out in the sun, and on windy days spray floats towards you like bubbles, or else you sit behind the large picture windows. If you prefer to choose your own lobster, you climb down a steep ladder to their wave-fed grotto. Always open. AE, DC, MC.

Loures (Lisbon). **Restaurant.** *Horta* (M), Rua dos Bombeiros Voluntarios 2 (tel. 9833804). 6 km. (4 miles) north of Lisbon, specializing in roast kid, also duck; *tipico* ambience. Delightful. Kitchen in view. Closed Wed.

Monte Estoril (Lisbon). Between Estoril proper and Cascais; as its name implies, it's hilly. *Atlantico* (E), Estrada Marginal (tel. 2680270). 175 rooms with bath. Huge pool; the electric train runs between hotel and sea. AE, DC, MC, V. *Estoril Eden* (E), Ave. Saboia (tel. 2670573). 162 studio apartments. On sea above Estrada Marginal. 2 restaurants, 2 heated pools, health club, garage. AE, DC, MC, V. *Grande* (M), Ave. Saboia (tel. 2684609). 72 rooms with bath and balcony. A good oldtimer with restaurant, bar and heated pool. Good value. AE, DC, MC, V. *Zenith* (M), Rua Belmonte (tel. 2680202). 48 rooms with bath and balcony. Glorious view from top floor; pleasant bar, rather shallow pool, friendly. AE, DC, MC. *Apart-hotel Touring Estoril* (I), Rua do Viveiro (tel. 2683385). A complex of buildings with a large number of fully-furnished and service apartments. Between Monte Estoril and Estoril, 15 minutes' walk from the beach. Pool, bar, good restaurant. AE, DC, MC. *Londres* (I), Ave. Fausto Figueiredo 17 (tel. 2684245). 68 rooms with bath. Pool. AE, DC, MC, V.

Restaurants. *A Maré* (E), next to Hotel Atlantico, Estrada Marginal (tel. 2685570). Good food; open every day. AE, DC, MC, V. *Casa Pizza* (M), Rua do Viveiro. Good Italian food. *English Bar* (M), Ave. Saboia 9 (tel. 2681254). Good view over the beach; serves first-class food in a relaxed atmosphere. Parking. Closed Sun. AE, DC, MC. *Ferra Mulinhas* (M), Rua do Viveiro 5 (tel. 2680005). Closed Tues. AE, DC, MC, V. *Maggie's Coffee Lounge* (M), Ave. São Pedro 1. Tea, coffee, snacks. Friendly. Closed Mon. *Ray's Bar* (M), Ave. de Saboia 25 (tel. 2680106). No food. Always open from 6 P.M. *O Sinaleiro* (I), Ave. de Saboia 35 (tel. 2685439). Excellent food, very reasonable; try their chicken. Closed Mon.

Oeiras (Lisbon). *Catalezete Youth Hostel.*
Restaurant. *Adega Tipica* (I), Rua Marques de Pombal 18–22. Good country food; own wine. Recommended. Closed Sept.

Palmela (Setúbal). *Pousada do Castelo de Palmela* (L), tel. 2351226. 29 rooms with bath. One of Portugal's best, in splendid Templars' castle on high hill at end of the Arrábida range, overlooking Setúbal and River Sado to the south, Lisbon and the Tagus to the north. Pool. Don't leave anything in your car. AE, DC, MC, V.

Portinho D'Arrábida (Setúbal). *Residência Santa Maria da Arrábida* (M), tel. 065 2080527. 33 rooms with bath. Breakfast only. Very safe, sandy beach. Open June through Sept.
Restaurants. *Beira Mar* (I–M) and *Galeão* (I–M). Both on superb beach.

Praia Grande (Lisbon). *Hotel das Arribas* (I), (tel. 9292145). 50 rooms with bath. Pool. AE, DC, MC, V.

Queluz (Lisbon). **Restaurants.** *Cozinha Velha* (L), Palácio Nacional (tel. 950740). One of the best restaurants in the Lisbon region. The original kitchen of the Queluz Palace, it has retained its old fittings, including the spits for roasting oxen whole. Worth the expense. AE, DC, MC, V. *Quadriga* (I), Ave. Elias Garcia 114 (tel. 951611). Well-cooked, simple food. Closed Thurs.

Rio De Mouro (Lisbon). *Quinta da Fonte Nova* (E), Serradas (tel. 9260021). 5 double rooms with bath, pool, riding, tennis, dinner by request. A Country House.

São Pedro De Sintra (Lisbon), about 1 km. from Sintra. **Restaurants.** *Galeria Real* (M), tel. 9231661. Very popular for wedding receptions; surrounded by antique shops. Closed Tues. AE, DC, MC. *O Cantinho* (M), Largo da Feira (tel. 9230267). French cooking, exceptional house wine. Parking. Closed Mon. and dinner Thurs. AE, DC, MC. *Solar São Pedro* (M), Largo da Feira 12 (tel. 9231860). Very good cooking and wine. Parking. Closed Wed. Avoid 2nd and 4th Sundays, which are Fair Days, as there is no parking available. AE, DC, MC.

Sesimbra (Setúbal). *Hotel do Mar* (E), tel. 2233326. 120 rooms with bath and balcony. Sea view, pool, disco, intriguing architecture. Fills up, so make sure your booking is firm. AE, DC, MC. *Espadarte* (I), tel. 2233189. 80 rooms with bath. On the esplanade, rather noisy. Good food. DC, MC.
Restaurants. *Ribamar* (M), Largo do Fortaleza (tel. 2233107). Always open. AE, DC, MC. *Gary's Bar* (I–M). On the waterfront; fun, mostly for drinks but also for coffee and snacks.

Setúbal (provincial capital). *Pousada de São Filipe* (E), tel. 065 23844. 15 rooms with bath. In ancient castle out of town, with splendid view over River Sado. Don't leave anything in your car. AE, DC, MC, V. *Esperança* (I), Ave. Luisa Todi 220 (tel. 065 25151). 76 rooms with bath. AE, DC, MC. *Pensão Bocage* (P), Rua São Cristovão 14 (tel. 065 21809). 20 rooms with bath. 14 more in annex. Breakfast only. *Pensão Mar e Sol* (P), Ave. Luisa Todi 606 (tel. 065 33016). 31 rooms with bath. Breakfast only.
Restaurants. There are several good *tascas* or small (I) restaurants near the ferry station for Troia, as well as reasonable eating houses all over town. *A Roda* (E), Travessa Postijo do Cais 7 (tel. 065 29264). Elegant. Closed Mon. AE, DC, MC. *Bocage* (M), Rua Marquês do Faial 5 (tel. 065 22513). Good Portuguese food: try muscatel brandy and the sweet, fortified muscatel wine, both from the region. Closed Mon. dinner and Tues. AE, DC, MC. *Cactus* (M), Rua Vasco da Gama 83 (tel. 065 34687). AE, DC, MC. *O Tunel* (M), Praça Bocage 62 (tel. 065 22732). A brash restaurant, excellent for a reasonable meal. *O Retiro* (I). A shack under the trees, for grilled sardines and barbecued chicken *al fresco*. *Rio Azul* (I), Rua Guilherme Fernandes 44 (tel. 065 22828). Local spot with good steaks and seafood; good value, quite near pousada. Closed Wed. AE.

Sintra (Lisbon). *Palácio de Seteais* (L), tel. 9233200. 18 rooms with bath. Superb 18th-century palace with glorious view; delicious food. A mile out of Sintra, and ideal for lunch when visiting the Sintra area. Set meal with plenty of choice. AE, DC, MC, V. *Quinta da Capela* (M), Monserrate (tel. 9290170). 11 rooms with bath. Lovely country house in beautiful setting. Small pool, gym, sauna. No restaurant, but several in nearby Colares. Closed Dec. to Feb. MC. *Quinta de São Thiago* (M), Monserrate (tel. 9232923). All rooms with bath. English owners take guests into their lovely 16th-century house. Pool. Meals. *Tivoli Sintra* (M), Praça da Republica (tel. 9233505). 75 rooms with bath; 5 suites. Good food and very reasonable winter terms. AE, DC, MC, V. *Central* (I), Praça da Republica 35 (tel. 9230963). 11 rooms with bath. In main square overlooking palace; large terrace; comfortable. *Pensão Sintra* (P), Travessa dos Avelares (tel. 9230738). 10 rooms with bath. *Pensão Nova Sintra* (P), Largo Afonso de Albuquerque 25 (tel. 9230220). 13 rooms. In pleasant villa. Up flight of steps to lovely terrace. Very reasonable, friendly.

Restaurants. There are several small restaurants. *Apeadeira* (I), Ave. Miguel Bombarda 3. Good food and wine. Closed Thurs. *Tulhas Bar* (I), Rua Gil Vicente 4. With good food and house wine. Closed Wed. AE, DC.

Troia (Setúbal). 12 minutes by car ferry from Setúbal. The *Torralta Complex* is huge and super-modern, with kindergarten, babysitting service; open-air theater; cafeteria and reasonably priced restaurants, pool. Long, attractive beaches; golf course designed by Robert Trent Jones. There are three apartment hotels: *Magnoliamar* (M), *Rosamar* (I), and *Tulipamar* (I), tel. 065 44151/44221. AE, DC, MC.

CAMPING. There are campsites at the following places: Cascais (Guincho/Orbitur); Costa da Caparica (6 different sites); Lagoa de Albufeira (2 sites); Lisbon (Monsanto); Oeiras; Palmela; Praia Grande (Colares); Sesimbra (3 sites); Setúbal (1 site); Sintra (Capuchos); Troia (Torralta); Vila Fresca de Azeitão.

POLLUTION REPORT. Unfortunately this area has a serious pollution problem because its sewage system is inadequate. The water off nine of the beaches between Lisbon, Estoril and Cascais has levels of pollution far above those permitted by the E.E.C. The problem is a long-standing one brought about by the development of the area, and there have been outbreaks of gastric disorders and skin infections for many years. At long last, a sewage treatment plant is to be built in Cascais, and the treated water will be carried far out to sea in an underwater pipe. Meanwhile, we strongly advise you not to use any beach in the area unless it has been officially declared safe.

PLACES OF INTEREST. Museums are usually open daily, except Mondays and public holidays, 10–5, but double check the times on the spot. Some close for lunch. Entrance fees are between 150$00 and 300$00.

Almada. Municipal Museum, Convento do Capuchos. Arabic archeology and tiles, 18th-century tiled panel depicting St. Francis of Assisi, paintings.

Alverca. Museu do Ar (Museum of Aviation). Full-size and scale model planes, helicopters and gliders.

Azeitão. Bacalhoa, Vila Fresca de Azeitão. Gardens open Mon. to Sat. 1–5; closed Sun. and Bank Holidays. Tip 200$00. Ring at gate along narrow entry overhung with bushes, opposite bus station. Also at Vila Fresca de Azeitão, the small São Simão tile factory. Friendly staff willing to explain the art.

Caparica. Municipal Museum, Convento de Madre de Deus (Convent of the Mother of God). 15th- and 16th-century ceramics, 17th- and 19th-century glass and local craftsmanship displayed in convent built in the 16th century by Franciscan monks and rebuilt in the 18th century.

Cascais. Museum and Library Condes dos Castro Guimarães, Furniture, paintings and books. Ethnographic and Cultural Section with agricultural utensils, regional costumes, earthenware, tiles, coins, and archeological remains. Library has English section.
Boca do Inferno. Deep chasm in the rocks with a whirlpool in rough weather.

Moita. Igreja da Nossa Senhora da Boa Viagem (Church of Our Lady of the Safe Journey). Rebuilt at the end of the 17th century, and containing several fine paintings on wood, gilded altars and 18th-century tiles.

Monserrate. Eccentric buildings and famous gardens. Between Sintra and Colares. Open daily 10–6.

Montijo. Igreja do Espirito Santo (Church of the Holy Spirit). 14th-century church with two beautiful classic portals of the early 17th century, 17th-century tiles, and gilded altars.
Igreja da Nossa Senhora da Atalaia. Pilgrimage church with 18th-century tiles; ex-votos. Romaria late June.

Odrinhas. Archeological Museum. Roman and Early Christian remains in the open air. Closed for lunch 12–2. Adm. free.

Palmela. Templar's Castle. Crowning high hill, partly a pousada.

Porto Salvo, Paço d'Arcos. Small archeological collections from Roman ruins nearby.

Queluz. Royal Palace. Mid-18th century palace with decorative art and furniture, *Arraiolos* carpets, Chinoiserie glazed tiles, and royal portraits. Lovely gardens. Closed Tues.

Rinchoa. Museu Leal da Camara (Leal da Camara Museum). Paintings and drawings of regional farmers, as well as paintings of Paris, by Leal da Camara.

Santa Susana, near Odrinhas. Small museum of pottery figures of country folk by artisan, Snr. Eduardo Azenha, who also sells his work.

São Domingos De Benfica. Palácio de Fronteira. Lovely formal gardens and notable private house. Open Sat. 1–5, Mon. 10–12 and 2:30–5.

First Sun. of the month, 2:30–5. Entrance to gardens only, 300$00. Gardens and house 1,000$00. Bus No. 46.

Seixal. Church. With lovely 17th-century panels and *azulejos.*
Ecomuseu Municipal. See the tidal water mill now working again.

Sesimbra. Municipal Museum. Archeology, numismatics, ethnographics and sacred art.

Setúbal. Archeology and Ethnography Museum. With section devoted to fishing traditions of the region and miniatures of ships.
Convento de Jesus. Contains examples of 15th-, 16th- and 17th-century architecture, paintings and examples of the goldsmith's art, as well as 14th-century documents and a library of 12,000 volumes including 16th-century first editions and valuable collection of autographs.
Oceanography and Fishing Museum. A valuable collection of marine species.

Sintra. Library and Historical Archives, Palace of Valenças. Collection of Romantic engravings of the 19th century, general literature and manuscripts.
Museum Anjos Teixeira. Statues, bronzes and other sculpture.
Museum Ferreira de Castro. Collection of this well-known Portuguese author's writings and his library.
Palácio Nacional (National Palace). In the town center, built on the site of a Moorish palace; with architectural features from the Arab to the Edwardian eras; lovely painted ceilings and beautiful furniture. Closed Wed.
Palácio da Pena (Palace of Pena). Unique example of 19th-century Portuguese Romantic architecture, with good decorative art, especially porcelain and furniture. Superb park with rare trees and shrubs. Closed Mon.
Regional Museum. Archeological and ethnographical exhibits.

ESTORIL CASINO. The Estoril Casino (tel. 2684521) is designed round a central patio, has deep upholstered sofas and chairs, not unlike a comfortable modern hotel lounge. There is also a red-and-gold nightclub with floorshows, a restaurant, comfortable cinema with afternoon and evening films, and in August a concert and ballet season. There are also frequent exhibitions by modern artists.

In the gambling rooms (note: take your passport) you can play roulette, boule, baccarat and craps. There is a special salon for slot machines, and one for bingo. Not smart; ample parking. Open 3 P.M.–3 A.M. AE, DC, MC.

SPECIAL EVENTS. The following are some of the many events taking place in this area. Check dates with Tourist Offices. **February.** During the 3 days of carnival before Ash Wednesday, gala balls are held nightly at the Estoril Casino. **May.** At Penha Longa, between Estoril and Sintra, a Country Fair is held on the Monday after Pentecost; music and dancing go on into the night. **June.** The annual fair of São Pedro takes place on June 29 at São Pedro de Sintra (where large fairs are also held on the 2nd and 4th Sundays of each month).

July. The *Feira do Artesanato* is held at Estoril (continuing into August)—an excellent occasion to enjoy regional specialties like the näive colorful pottery from Portugal's northern provinces. Taste regional fare and wines at the many restaurants or just sample country bread hot from an old-fashioned kiln. Music and ballet festival in Casino. The *Feira de Sant'Iago* at Setúbal, end of month, includes various exhibitions of the region's agro-industrial activities, a funfair, folklore dancing and other attractions.

August. At Alcochete, in the 2nd week of Aug. are the festivals of the *Barrete Verde* (green cap) and the *Salinas,* with bullfights and outdoor celebrations. (Take the ferry to Montijo, then the bus.) On Aug. 17 at Janas (about 15 minutes' drive from Sintra) the day of the patron saint, São Mamede, is celebrated: animals are blessed after their three tours round the unique, pre-Roman circular chapel; pottery and fairings are laid out on the grass.

September. The *Festa das Vindimas* (Feast of the Grape Harvest) takes place at Palmela, with symbolic treading of the grapes and the blessing of the must, dancing, folklore, fireworks, winetasting and, on the last night, the castle of Palmela is burnt in effigy; end of month.

SHOPPING. The area around Lisbon can provide a wide range of shopping opportunities, from the smart boutiques of Cascais to the simple crafts deep in the heart of the countryside. **Crafts.** Estoril offers good quality merchandise: for reasonably priced country goods and embroideries, try *Regionalia,* 27 Arcadas do Parque; for filigree jewelry, *M. Fernandes,* Hotel Palácio. In Cascais, the *Cestaria de Cascais,* Rua Visconde da Luz 5, is devoted to baskets and basket work of all kinds—a fascinating display; *Bagatelle,* Ave. 25 de Abril, is an excellent little shop for pretty gifts in porcelain and silver plate.

Try bargaining for a pretty tablecloth at the stalls by the harbor. On the road between Sintra and Mafra, the visitor passes through the town of Pero Pinheiro. On both sides of the road large slabs of marble are stacked. At *Pardal Monteiro Ltd.,* visitors are welcome to watch the fascinating work of cutting and polishing. Marble objects, such as ashtrays, bought or ordered at the source are amazingly inexpensive.

Fashion. In Cascais, hosts of small boutiques have sprung up, particularly in the smart pedestrian Rua Frederico Arouca. Look out for *Gloria's* at No. 55 for good clothes, *Perfumaria Katinka* at No. 37 for scents, face creams, etc., and *Peacock,* opposite, for belts and handbags. Near the market, at Ave. 25 de Abril 10A, is *Tara,* a teenager's heaven for ready-made dresses and slacks.

Flowers. Flowers for gifts to others or for yourself can be bought from the shop in the western Arcade in Estoril, or on the Estrada Marginal 2 in Cascais. The most reasonable flower shop is in the Pão de Açucar supermarket on the Estrada Marginal at the entrance to Cascais. But naturally, flowers are cheaper in the Cascais market, open till 2 every afternoon except Sundays.

Food. The best days to visit Cascais market are Wednesday and Saturday, when the country people come in and mounds of newly gathered fruit and vegetables are piled on the ground. Bargaining is expected, the final price being often three quarters of that originally asked.

Among the many supermarkets, perhaps the best is *Espaçial,* Ave. Biarritz 12, Estoril. Prices are lowest at the huge *Pão de Açucar,* Estrada Marginal 6, Cascais, which also has 2 cinemas and a number of smart shops on the 1st floor.

SPORTS. The area is full of opportunities for the sports enthusiast. There are many specialist clubs and some have facilities for several sports. The *Quinta da Marinha* club (tel. 289881), past Cascais on the Guincho road, has a new 18-hole golf course designed by Robert Trent Jones, as well as two pools, tennis, equestrian center, and restaurant. On the same road, available to visitors as well as members, is the *Clube de Campo D. Carlos I* (tel. 2852362), a pine-covered property offering a very pleasant heated swimming pool, sauna, tennis courts, and riding.

Golf. *Lisbon Sports Club,* Belas (tel. 960077); *Quinta da Marinha* (see above); *Clube de Golfe do Estoril* (tel. 2680176), which rents all equipment and has a restaurant and pool (turn off at signpost on Ave. Sintra); a new nine-hole course at Linhó (tel. 9232461), between Estoril and Sintra; *Troia Golf Club,* Troia (tel. 065 44151), 18-hole course in splendid country on River Sado.

Riding. *Centro Hipico de Cascais,* Quinta da Guia (tel. 2843563). *Centro Hipico da Costa do Estoril,* Charneca, Cascais (tel. 2852064). *Centro Hipico da Quinta da Marinha,* Cascais (tel. 289282). *Centro Hipico de Campo D. Carlos I,* Quinta da Marinha, Cascais (tel. 2851403). *Escola de Equitacão da Areia,* Cascais (tel. 289284). *Pony Club,* Quinta da Bicuda, Torre, Cascais (tel. 2843058).

Tennis. *Lisbon Sports Club,* Belas (tel. 960077); *Clube de Campo D. Carlos* (see above); *Grupo Desportivo de Pescadores,* Costa da Caparica (tel. 2904110); *Clu-be de Ténis do Jamor,* Estadio Nacional, Cruz Quebrada (tel. 2112147); *Hotel de Turismo de Ericeira,* Ericeira (tel. 061 63545); *Clube de Ténis do Estoril,* Ave. Amaral, Estoril (tel. 2681675); *Grande Hotel,* Estoril (tel. 2684609); *Hotel Sintra Estoril,* on road to Sintra (tel. 2690721); *Clube Montijense de Desportos,* Montijo; *Clube Escola de Ténis de Oeiras,* Oeiras (tel. 2436699); *Clube de Ténis de Setúbal,* Setúbal (tel. 065 27038); *Parque das Merendas,* Sintra (tel. 9232800); *Apartamentos Turisticos Torralta,* Troia (tel. 065 44151).

Sailing. *Clube Naval Barreirense,* Barreiro (tel. 2073779); *Club Naval de Cascais,* Cascais (tel. 280125); *Associação Naval de Lisboa,* Lisbon (tel. 600488); *Clube Naval de Lisboa,* Lisbon (tel. 369354); *Clube Naval de Sesimbra,* Sesimbra (tel. 2233451); *Clube Naval Setubalense,* Setúbal (tel. 065 22756).

Windsurfing. *Escola de Carcavelos de Windsurfing,* Carcavelos (tel. 2470113); *Clube Naval de Cascais,* Cascais (tel. 280125); *Windsurfing Center Cascais,* Cascais (tel. 2841736); *International Windsurfing School,* Estoril (tel. 2681665); Praia de Santa Cruz, tel. 061 23094.

TOURS AND EXCURSIONS. *Tip Tours,* Ave. Costa Pinto 91A, Cascais (tel. 283821), have bus excursions to Lisbon, Fatima, Alcobaça, Batalha, and other places, picking up passengers at hotels. They also hire out bicycles and arrange deep-sea fishing expeditions.

USEFUL ADDRESSES. Travel Agents. *American Express,* Star Travel Service, Ave. de Nice 4, Estoril (tel. 2680839 and 2681945); *Wagons*

Lits/Cooks, Aracadas do Parque, Estoril (tel. 2680225); *Agencic Abreu,* Galerias Estoril-Sol Cascais (tel. 280861).

Car Hire. *Avis,* Tamariz, Estoril (tel. 2685728); *Rent-a-Car Guérin,* Cruzeiro, Estoril (tel. 2680066).

Villa Hire. *Cicerone,* Ave. Bombeiros Voluntarios 6, Estoril (tel. 2680389).

Bank. Lloyds Bank plc., Ave. de São Pedro 1, Monte Estoril, Estoril (tel. 2670536).

Club. *American Women of Lisbon Club,* Ave. de Sintra 3, Cascais (tel. 280252). Friendly group including other nationalities; numerous activities, library, meals. Also has a few rooms with bath.

Churches. St. Paul's Anglican Church, Ave. Bombeiros Voluntarios 1C, Estoril (tel. 2683570); Corpo Santo Parish Center (R.C.), Rua do Murtal 368, São Pedro do Estoril (tel. 2681676); Mass is also said on Sun. midday in St. Sebastian's Chapel, Parque de Castro Guimarães, Cascais.

THE PORTUGUESE EPIC

A mild, salubrious climate on the coast of a sea teeming with fish; great rivers, beautiful forests and deep, sheltered valleys; few carnivorous beasts or poisonous snakes—everything about Portugal favored a flourishing primitive existence whose only remaining traces are ancient idols, Iron Age settlements, dolmens, and mounds of seashells along the shores. The dark-skinned, thick-set Iberians were the primary racial strain in a widely scattered population; later, as a result of foreign trade and invasions, their blood would mingle with that of the Celts, the Phoenicians, Jews and Moors, all of whom were easily absorbed as can be seen in the faces of the Portuguese men and women of today.

Until the middle of the 12th century A.D., the history of Portugal is one with the general history of the Iberian Peninsula. For the Ancients, Cape St. Vincent in the province of Algarve marked the end of the earth, for there they could see the sun swallowed up by the sea. Not far away, the commercially-minded Carthaginians and Greeks set up trading posts on Portugal's southern shore.

The Romans annexed the Iberian Peninsula, with its wealth of olive oil and wine, around 200 B.C. Whereas Gaul had been quickly conquered and Romanized, Lusitania mounted a stubborn resistance. A chieftain from the hills named Viriathus, the Hannibal of the Iberians as Lucilius said, held the Roman legions at bay for years; he embodied the ferocious attachment to the native soil and the blind, desperate heroism which have always been constant factors in the history of Portugal.

Rome's relationship with her far-off province was one of exploitation rather than development. She did, however, construct roads, bridges and aqueducts, some of which still exist; she also founded cities, of which nothing remains today but their names. The beautiful Temple of Diana at Evora and, above all, the ruins of Conimbriga, near Coimbra, which had been buried for centuries, bear witness to an affluent and peaceful lifestyle. Christianity easily took root in such soil. The bishopric of Braga was established as early as the third century.

The Invasions

Then came the Barbarians. At Conimbriga, a hastily built wall (you can still see the broken statues and columns of porphyry used to fortify it) failed to protect the city against the onslaught of the Suevi. The next invaders, the Visigoths, imposed a warlike regime but, little by little, they were won over by the pious and pastoral existence of the people they thought they had conquered. By the sixth century, the Church had greatly increased its influence and chapels and monasteries sprang up on the banks of the Douro and the Mondego rivers.

Wamba, the 30th king of the Visigoths who had reluctantly accepted the crown in 672, demanded to be consecrated at Toledo. He repulsed an invasion force of 260 ships which the Moors, Turks and Arabs, the new masters of North Africa, launched against the peninsula. After Wamba's death, quarrels among the barons and the criminal spite of Julian (who had betrayed the invasion route to Tariq, the Emir of Africa) enabled the Moors to defeat Rodrigo, last king of the Goths, at Guadalete in the year 711. Rodrigo took refuge in a hermitage on the Asturian coast, and the Moorish tide rolled on as far north as Poitiers. Alone, a small band of Christian noblemen under the leadership of Pelayo entrenched themselves in the mountains of Asturias and began the arduous reconquest which was to endure for centuries.

The Moorish domination of Portugal was fruitful: orchards sprang up from irrigated land, indeed, their methods of irrigation are still being used in Portugal today; white and fawn-colored cities came to life and prospered. The tolerant Moors welcomed Jews and even protected the studious meditations of Christian monks. A Moorish–Arabian culture spread outward from the cities of Coimbra and Kelb, now Silves in the Algarve. The very name Algarve is a Moorish survival, it was originally al-Gharb.

First Dynasty: the House of Burgundy (the Founders)

Meanwhile, north of the River Douro, Christian counts and barons from Galicia, León and Asturias kept watch and waited for an opportunity to renew the offensive which had already enabled them to liberate Burgos, Toledo and Santiago de Compostela. Portugal was about to be born as a separate country at the height of the 12th century, amid the bellicose and religious exaltation of the reconquest.

The younger sons of the great families left frequently to fight abroad. The excitement of the Crusades drew many of them to the Holy Land; however, some of them considered that it was more important to liberate Europe and to hurl the Infidel back into the sea before setting out to rescue the Holy Sepulcher. The Cid captured Valencia. Among his comrades-in-arms was a Count of Burgundy who had received the hand in marriage of one of the daughters of the King of León in Spain for services rendered.

Her dowry consisted of lands located between the Douro and the Minho rivers, at that time a country called Portucale. Their son, Afonso Henriques, seized the throne from his regent mother in 1128. He freed himself by pushing the Moors to the south.

With foolhardy courage, and seconded by knights cut from the same cloth as himself, Afonso captured seven Moorish strongholds—a feat he commemorated by incorporating them into the Portuguese coat-of-arms. You can see the ramparts of these fortresses today at Lisbon, Leiria, Santarém, Sintra, Palmela, Montemor and Evora.

Afonso's descendants brought order to their kingdom, defending and enlarging its frontiers. Dom Dinis, the poet-king, founded the University of Coimbra in 1308 and built the first Portuguese fleet. He had pine trees planted in the sandy soil between the sea and Leiria, dominated by his hill-top castle, in order to stabilize the land and conserve the crops. He married Isabella, the Infanta of Aragon, later known as St. Elizabeth of Portugal for her devotion and concern for the poor. Her piety is celebrated in many legends, mostly concerning the conversion of gold to roses and vice versa. Apart from the one we have already related in the Introduction, there was the occasion, upon completion of the Church of Santa Clara-a-Velha which she had ordered built in Coimbra, when she had nothing but a rose to offer the workmen as payment—which turned to gold in their hands.

The son of this Holy Queen was the stormy Prince Afonso, whose rebellion darkened the last years of his father's reign. After Afonso became king, he received the same kind of treatment at the hands of his own progeny. He gave his son Pedro in marriage to Constança, a princess of Navarre. Constança had a beautiful Galician friend and cousin named Inês de Castro as a lady-in-waiting. Inês and Prince Pedro soon became entwined in an ill-fated affair. Constança died alone and unloved in giving birth to a son, but Pedro cared only for the children presented him by Inês, whose brothers were adept in the art of courtly intrigue. Their ambitions frightened the old King Afonso, whose councillors pressed him to sacrifice Inês in the interests of the kingdom. He resigned himself to the bitter necessity of this course of action and had her murdered in the garden of the Quinta das Lágrimas in Coimbra. The stones in the spring by which she died show dusky red through the bright water to this day. After Inês's death, when Pedro became king, he wreaked a horrible vengeance upon her murderers, and crowned her corpse before having it transported to Alcobaça in a great funeral procession. She was laid to rest in a magnificent tomb which Pedro ordered to be placed opposite his own so that the first sight each should see on the Day of Resurrection would be the beloved face of the other. The last of the Burgundians died with no male heir, and the King of Castile marched on Lisbon with a powerful army to back up his claim to the throne.

Second Dynasty: the House of Aviz (the Explorers)

The threatened capital placed itself in the hands of João, one of Pedro's illegitimate sons, who was head of the military and religious Order of Aviz. He was named Defender of the Realm, and then elected king by popular acclaim. All Portugal united around him to preserve its independence. Lisbon suffered a cruel siege; but then, led by João I and his young captain

Nuno Álvares Pereira, the Portuguese army fought courageously in a clash with the Castilian cavalry. The battle took place on August 14, 1385, on the Plain of Aljubarrota, and 14,000 Portuguese infantry and crossbowmen with 3,000 English archers and horsemen routed 30,000 Castilian soldiers and horsemen. This battle secured the independence of Portugal for almost two centuries. The spoils of victory were immense. As an act of gratitude for his victory, João erected the monastery of Nossa Senhora da Vitória at Batalha, not far from the battlefield. He was later buried there with his wife, Philippa of Lancaster, daughter of John of Gaunt; their marriage confirmed the Portuguese pact with England—the oldest continuing alliance in Europe. This Treaty of Windsor, signed in 1386, was invoked by Britain in World War II to obtain fueling facilities for ships and aircraft in the Azores Archipelago, which were duly granted. The sixth centenary of the treaty in 1986 was widely commemorated in both countries.

Philippa bore six children to João, one of whom, the Infanta Isabella, married Philip of Burgundy, Grand Duke of the Occident. But the most famous of this "noble generation" was Henry the Navigator. His wise and learned face appears in the celebrated polyptych in the *Lisbon Art Gallery* painted by Nuno Gonçalves, a disciple of Van Eyck.

After having played an important role in the conquest of Ceuta in 1415, Henry retired to the arid promontory of Sagres, in Algarve, where he surrounded himself with seamen, map-makers and astronomers. Using their vast experience and original calculations, these scholars at Sagres were the first to establish the principles of navigation on the high seas. Here also the caravelle was developed—the first sailing ship capable of being navigated in a cross wind. None of these long-range expeditions would have been possible without the painstaking and inspired research of Henry, the "Prince of the Sea."

The Atlantic archipelagos (Madeira in 1420 and the Azores in 1431) were the first discoveries of Henry's explorers; the latter were colonized for a while by the Flemish, after Faial had been given to Isabella of Burgundy in 1466. These islands proved to be excellent stepping stones for the exploration of the west coast of Africa. Henry, unlike Columbus, was certain that a sea route to India could be found by circumnavigating this still-unknown continent.

The caravans from the Orient, which carried the precious stones, spices, silks and gold of which Europe had always been so fond, were becoming exposed to ever-increasing dangers. Although their safe conduct had previously been assured by paying protection money to the Arabs of the Middle East and the pirates of the Mediterranean, the caravans now found themselves subject to attacks by the Turks.

It was therefore of vital importance to the European economy to have direct access to those countries that produced spices, silk and gold.

The Discoveries

Christopher Columbus, who had lived for over a year on the island of Porto Santo off Madeira, and who had often sailed with Prince Henry's captains, sought this mythical westward route to India (on the last and most desolate of the islands of the Azores, a mysterious weathered stone still points toward the setting sun). It was while seeking this route to India that Columbus accidentally discovered America in 1492.

Bartolomeu Dias rounded the Cape of Storms at the southern tip of Africa in 1488, 28 years after the Navigator's death; it was immediately rechristened Cape of Good Hope, since this momentous event confirmed the certitude of Henry and his followers that here indeed lay the route to India and the Spice Islands. Finally, in 1498, Vasco da Gama reached Calcutta.

Portuguese explorations opened up a multitude of new worlds to the Old World. In 1500 Pedro Álvares Cabral discovered Brazil. The following year Corte-Réal landed at Greenland, while Cabrilo and João Martins explored the coasts of California and Alaska, respectively. The Portuguese were the first white men to reach the Moluccas, China, Japan and Ethiopia and, thanks to the voyage of Magellan in 1520, the first to circumnavigate the globe.

An immense Portuguese empire now spread over four continents. Missionaries like St. Francis Xavier and Father Manuel de Nobrega carried the word of Christ into the jungles and the deserts, to pagan tribes and to the ancient civilizations of Asia. Trading posts were established in Guinea, Malacca, Ceylon and Oceania; fortresses were built to protect them, and a Portuguese monopoly was maintained throughout the Indian Ocean—often at a bloody price.

Nevertheless, the great Afonso of Albuquerque was not as proud of having conquered Ormuz and Malacca as he was of having founded at Malabar a new race of Christians—the Luso-Hindus of Goa. In the Congo, 12 Christian churches graced the city of San Salvador, capital of the black King Afonso (godson and ally of the King of Portugal). Everywhere—from Madeira to Macau, where Portugal had established the first European settlement in China in 1557, from Cape Verde to Mozambique—Portuguese was spoken by a mixture of races, making it the universal language of the time. Hundreds of Portuguese words are still found today in many of the dialects of Africa and Asia.

The Lisbon of Manuel the Fortunate

Lisbon had gotten the better of its major commercial rivals: first Bruges, then Venice. It was the richest city of Europe. Using revenues from the lucrative tax on pepper, King Manuel (called "the Fortunate Monarch") built the church and monastery of the Jeronimites at Belém on the same shore from which Vasco da Gama had set sail. Manuel chose the armillary sphere as his emblem, to indicate that his realm extended around the world—or at least a good half-way around the world, since a treaty signed at Tordesillas with Spain (and confirmed by the Pope) had divided the new world between them: the two spheres of influence were defined by a line passing 370 leagues to the west of Cape Verde.

Intoxicated with the riches of this universal empire, Portugal decorated buildings and public monuments with emblems of its conquests on the high seas and in the jungles of the tropics: representations of anchors, seaweed and rigging mingled with exotic animals and strange symbols. Belém, Batalha, Tomar—all bear witness, sculptured in stone, to the fact that the Portuguese of the 16th century envisioned their empire as a grand fusion of diverse races and civilizations, with Christianity and the Portuguese language as their common bond.

This sudden prosperity of Portugal was, like its new-found power, more apparent than real. Their senses reeling with the spirit of adventure, the Portuguese lost sight of the more solid virtues of their race: endurance, sobriety and tolerance. They wasted their wealth in idle luxury, cultivating a false pride fraught with danger for the future.

King Sebastian, the frail and unstable end-product of a once great but now worn-out bloodline (he was the grandson of the flamboyant Manuel and the all-powerful Charles V of Spain), hurled himself into an absurd and fatal crusade in Morocco (1578). During the massacre of Al-Kebir, the king perished along with the flower of the country's youth. This event left Portugal ruined and drained of its last drop of royal blood—an easy prey for its powerful neighbor, Spain.

Camões, the great Portuguese poet who had sung of the era of discovery in his *Lusiads,* died the same year that Portugal fell into the hands of Philip II of Spain; his last words are said to have been, "I am dying at the same time as my country."

Third Dynasty: the House of Bragança (the Restoration)

The Spanish domination lasted for 60 years. The three Philips who wore this double crown cared little about the interests of Portugal, who lost many of her overseas possessions and was dragged into all of Spain's quarrels—with France, with Holland, and even with England, Portugal's traditional ally.

In 1640, with the overwhelming support of popular opinion and the approval of the various enemies of Madrid, a group of Portuguese patriots expelled the Spanish. They installed on the throne the most powerful nobleman in Portugal, the Duke of Bragança—descended from the old royal family through his grandmother—who took the title of João IV. During his entire reign he had to contend with the armed intervention of Spain. Six years after his death in 1656, his widow confirmed Portugal's alliance with England by giving their daughter, Catherine, in marriage to Charles II.

These constant wars ruined the country, but the unswerving loyalty of the Brazilian colony retained for Portugal a source of gold, diamonds and precious wood. João V helped himself to this wealth with both hands: he launched dazzling projects, such as the Aqueduct of the Free Waters in Lisbon; heedless of cost, he erected buildings on an irrationally grand scale, the monastery at Mafra and the University Library at Coimbra among them. The Chapel of St. John the Baptist in Lisbon's Church of St. Roque, constructed mainly of lapis lazuli, is another example of the appetite for magnificence of the Maecenas-like king. He was infatuated with foreign styles: his architects were Italian or German, while his furniture and tableware came from France. Grotesque though his extravagance was, this prodigal king added many churches and Baroque palaces to the architectural wealth of Portugal.

The Earthquake

João V had been dead for five years when, on November 1, 1755, a terrible earthquake shook the entire country and destroyed a large part of Lisbon. In the cruel years that followed, Pombal, a great statesman and powerful minister of King José I, succeeded in raising Portugal from its ruins. A cruel and unrelenting but enlightened despot, Pombal held the nobility in check, limited the power of the church (expelling the Jesuits), and breathed new life into commerce and industry. He rebuilt Lisbon in the beautiful, austere architecture clearly derived from the Queen Anne style in London, where Pombal had served as Portuguese Minister, but here lightened by the local temperament. The streets between the Rossio and the great colonnaded riverside square, the Praça do Comércio, or Terreiro do Paço are an early example of town planning and show one facet of Pombal's many-sided genius. After the death of José I, Pombal fell into disgrace; his religious changes were overturned by the new, pious queen, and he died in the town which bears his name.

In the years covering the turn of the century, the Peninsular War (1808–14) proved crucial to Napoleon's fortunes. In order to deprive England of her overseas naval bases, he invaded Portugal on three separate occasions. Under the generalship of Sir Arthur Wellesley, later the Duke of Wellington, Britain carried the war into Portugal itself, and, after a series of hard-fought campaigns from 1808–11, the French were finally forced to retire, as much by starvation as by the force of arms. The war shifted over into Spain, and Portuguese troops fought side by side with the British until Napoleon was at last defeated.

After the Peninsular War, Napoleon left the country devastated and vulnerable to the destructive influences of internal strife. João VI was in Brazil for most of his reign, during which his younger son Miguel plotted against his elder brother Pedro, and started a civil war. But on the accession of the young Maria II in 1826, Miguel was made regent; he then usurped the throne, causing further strife until he was expelled from the country in 1834. The monarchy had by now become unpopular; it was blamed for all the ills of a country which had been abandoned to political intrigue.

While Portugal was thus wasting away, the other European powers were actively seeking new outlets for their commerce—especially in Africa. England decided to unite Africa from the Cape to Cairo. At the Congress of Berlin, France, Prussia and Italy divided among themselves a continent in which Leopold of Belgium had taken the lion's share. In order to pacify the Bantu tribesmen, who had risen, being cleverly manipulated and armed by outside interests, troops were sent from Portugal to reinforce the local garrisons in Angola and Mozambique.

In Lisbon, popular agitation reached fever pitch. On February 1, 1908, King Carlos and Crown Prince Luis were assassinated by anarchists on the Terreiro do Paço. Two years later the monarchy, in the person of Manuel II, was overturned, the Bragança family was banished, and a republic proclaimed. Manuel withdrew to England where he lived in retirement until his death in 1932, leaving all his properties in Portugal back to the State. These properties, notably the palace and chase at Vila Viçosa are managed by an independent body, the Casa de Bragança.

However, simply becoming a republic did not restore peace and prosperity. A costly and confused participation in World War I (in Africa and northern France) at the request of the Allies, further aggravated Portugal's social and economic problems.

The Modern State

Between 1911 and 1926, 44 governments attempted to raise the country from the morass into which it had sunk. A *coup d'état* in 1926 brought General Gomes da Costa to power as President, followed by General Carmona—the latter retained the nation's confidence until his death in 1951. He appealed to António de Oliveira Salazar, professor of political economy in the Law Faculty at the University of Coimbra, to rebuild the national economy and take Portugal's destiny in hand. From 1928, first as Minister of Finance, then as Prime Minister, Salazar was in effective charge of the country, maintaining a parallel dictatorship to Franco's in next door Spain. After having maintained, in the face of many pitfalls and calculated risks, an active neutrality during World War II, Portugal made considerable economic progress, but at the expense of any social modernization.

After suffering a severe stroke in 1968, Dr. Salazar was succeeded, after a constructive dictatorship of almost 40 years, by Dr. Marcello Caetano, a Professor of Law at Lisbon University. Caetano was respected and might have been able to bring his country into a more democratic way of life had he had the courage to replace the then President, Admiral Americo Tomas, by a man more aware of the problems caused by the 13 years of colonial war, waged to retain control of Portugal's great African empire of Angola and Mozambique. Although fatal casualties were remarkably few, many members of the armed forces were injured by landmines and boobytraps, which did not improve morale and both the privates and officers were very badly paid.

So it was not surprising that a military uprising took place in the mother country, led by 64-year-old General António de Spinola in April 1974. This Carnation Revolution—so called because the soldiers put red carnations in the barrels of their rifles—was a bloodless one, fewer than 20 people being killed, and those almost by accident, in the few disturbances which ensued. Spinola was appointed President of a predominantly Left-wing government, but he was shortly replaced and banished to Brazil where Marcello Caetano and Admiral Américo Tomás had been allowed to go directly after the coup. Both former Presidents were allowed back into Portugal, where Admiral Américo Tomás died. Marcello Caetano returned to academic life in a Brazilian university and died in 1980.

Free elections have since shown that the great majority of the Portuguese people want to build a new nation in peace and on foundations of common sense. The massive aid and loans from the United States and other nations have largely revived the economy, and the election of a Social Democratic government by a large majority in 1987 augurs well for a better future.

Some 700,000 refugees, a large proportion of them black (which is a tribute to Portuguese rule overseas), poured into the country in 1975 from the African possessions which had been granted independence, and from Timor in the Far East, annexed by Indonesia. This is almost a tenth of the total population of the country. The government rapidly formed a special department to succor these unfortunate "returned ones" as they were called. At first those who had no relatives in Portugal were lodged free in hotels and boarding houses, but eventually those who had not found jobs and accommodation were moved to army barracks and unused buildings, so that tourism could get under way again, which it has done in a big way. Many of the refugees have started their own businesses and they are all becoming fully integrated.

Joining the European Common Market in 1986 would, it was believed, bring industry up to date and above all improve the very backward state of agriculture, which should be able to produce enough to feed the whole country. The condition of the people has greatly improved since the revolution in spite of unemployment. Wages have increased, inflation, which rocketed for some years, is slowing down, and the social services are improving, with health care operating all over the country and pensions for the disabled and elderly.

The really amazing thing is that a country so strictly controlled for over 40 years should burst into the light of free speech and free association with so little actual violence and bloodshed. It speaks well for the inherent qualities of the Portuguese people that, in spite of pressures from outside and hysteria from within, they are building themselves a place in the Europe of Today.

CREATIVE PORTUGAL

The Portuguese language, which is spoken today by over 100 million people in various parts of the world, never fails to astonish anyone who is hearing it for the first time. When the Romans conquered Lusitania some two centuries before the Christian era, they acquired the embryo of a nation; the desperate resistance of the soldiers of Viriathus, Chief of the Lusitanians, who had a fierce desire for independence, demonstrated a moral unit, a kind of ethnical solidarity. That solidarity grew during the fight against the Moors and brought about such a strong national consciousness that Portugal emerged from among the rival kingdoms fighting the Moors as a nation having exactly the same frontiers in 1139 as today.

Despite its Slavic-sounding inflections and nasal intonations, so elusive to the unpracticed ear, Portuguese is essentially a Romance language. The unity of the Portuguese language dates back to the 12th century. Henry of Burgundy—the father of Afonso Henriques, Portugal's first ruler—had brought with him to the peninsula a considerable retinue of French noblemen and scholars. No wonder that early Portuguese literature is like a renewal of Provençal poetry. At that time, the use of prose was restricted to the chronicling of historically significant events.

Sancho I, the son of Afonso Henriques, was a poet and, some 100 years later, Dom Dinis was also composing his love poetry and songs of friendship. Both of them had been taught by French troubadours. Duarte I, whose courtiers—including the ladies—were learned scholars, proficient in both Greek and Latin, developed a stricter literary form, the essay. Subsequently, there were the chronicles of Fernão Lopes, the historian of Portugal's tragic Middle Ages, and those of Azurara, who accompanied the explorers of Sagres in their wanderings.

Portuguese literature, as a diversion of princes, ran the risk of remaining too restrained and too affected, since the period demanded preoccupation with form. However, the 15th century brought to it what had been lacking—virility, strength, the discovery of new horizons, a taste for observation, and inspired exaltation. When Pedro Vaz da Caminha described the arrival of Pedro Alvares Cabral's ships in Brazil, he was merely reporting, but when, a half century later, Camões sang of the arrival of Vasco da Gama's fleet in India, he did so in an epic poem. The primary reason for the change is that during those 50 years Portugal had written one of the most extraordinary, romantic, and heroic chapters of history. Oceans were conquered, islands and lands discovered, and continents outlined.

Literature was inspired by the history with which everyone was surrounded. Great men of letters, such as Pedro Nunes, essayist and mathematician, André de Resende, humanist, Damião de Gois, historian, Sá de Miranda, poet, Bernardino Ribeiro, a poet who wrote a novel, António Ferreira, also a poet, and Fernão Mendes Pinto, adventurer, lived during this half-century and made it illustrious.

But not until Gil Vicente's time do we find a typically Portuguese lyric inspiration. His *autos,* or "mysteries," skillfully express many different kinds of themes, including the serious, the truculent, the heroic, and occasionally the prophetic. There are excellent translations available of his works. However, the outstanding representative of Portuguese literature is Luiz de Camões, a not unworthy contemporary of Cervantès and Shakespeare. The *Lusiads* sing of the people whose glory and wretchedness he shared: allegory and myth mingle with the prodigious epic of the Discoveries, blending facts, heroes, and legends into the masterpiece of a genius. However, many readers prefer—instead of the bright fanfare of the famous *Ten Songs*—the pure, artfully contrived harmonies of the *Sonnets,* tinged with melancholy, that sing so sweetly of love.

The Spanish domination between 1580 and 1640 naturally led to a decrease in Portuguese writing, though the Jesuit António de Vieira, who went to Brazil, wrote fascinating letters from that immense and then largely unexplored country. His work is now becoming a popular source of study among academics.

The *Love Letters from a Portuguese Nun* are imbued with love and sadness: they were supposedly written by Mariana Alcoforado, a nun at the Beja convent of Conceição, now a museum, to a dashing French officer. First published in France in 1669 and since translated into many languages, these letters remain a fascinating literary mystery. The Portuguese originals have never been found and little is known of either the writer or of the Chevalier de Chamilly, who is believed to have received these moving epistles.

Bocage, who died in 1805, was the leading satirical and lyric poet of the 18th century. He left some admirable sonnets conveying exquisite bitterness and despair. In the same century Francisco Manoel do Nascimento was an early opponent of rhyme in poetry.

The Romantic Movement came late to Portugal, only around 1825. The most brilliant of the writers of that time was Almeida Garrett, who died in 1854. He was not only a novelist and dramatist, but also a poet who influenced a whole generation in a century prolific in remarkable writers whose works are little known outside their own country. These include Camilo Castelo Branco and Julio Dinis, both novelists, the historians Alexandre Herculano and Oliveira Martins and the poets Antero de Quental and António de Castilho.

The latter half of the last century almost exactly covered the life of the greatest Portuguese novelist, Eça de Queiroz. He was an early realist and his books, all translated into English, are well worth reading for their brilliance and vivid writing.

Fernando Pessoa, who died in 1935, was a prolific poet, the author of diversified works distinguished by their classic form and by surrealistic flashes in their synthetic expression and imagery. His reputation is becoming established, and deservedly so, in many countries. His followers in the "modern movement" include José Regio, Almada Negreiros, Miguel Torga and Natalia Correia.

Mention must also be made of other writers who rank among the Portuguese classics, including Trindade Coelho, Ana de Castro Osório (Portugal's first woman novelist), Ferreira de Castro, Fernando Namora and Aquilino Ribeiro. Among contemporary writers are José Gomes Ferreira, Sofia de Melo Breyner, José Cardoso Pires, Joaquim Paço d'Arcos and Luis Sttau Monteiro. Although novelists have not yet found inspiration in the revolution of 1974, a great number of political studies have been published and several books of memoirs and autobiographies.

Architecture

The relics of the Roman occupation of Portugal are many though few have been excavated: splendid bridges (Chaves and Ponte de Lima), the old roadbeds, several thermal springs and, notably, the Evora temple (second-century), with its marble-topped granite colonnade. And at Conimbriga you will find intact the highly picturesque remains of a Lusitanian settlement looking much as it did before the barbarian hordes overran it. Prehistoric *citanias* or hill cities can still be seen in the north. The most fully excavated is that of Briteiros near Guimarães.

Many Visigothic vestiges remain: pilasters, columns, etc., in the museums. Although considerably damaged and inexpertly restored, St. Frutuoso, near Braga (seventh-century), stands out as the purest example of Byzantine art in the peninsula (it is laid out like a Greek cross). The Templars' Shrine at Tomar (12th-century) derives its octagonal shape from the temple of Jerusalem.

Portugal's churches mark the various stages in the process of reconquest during which the Christians gradually pushed the Moors southwards. Numerous Romanesque chapels, utterly touching in their humbleness, sturdy as the faith that inspired them, artlessly adorned with simply carved capitals and portals, cover the landscape between Minho and Douro, all the way to the Mondego. Those at Rates, Fonte Arcada and Bravães merit special consideration. The early bishops, who were often French, built cathedrals on the model of Cluny (notably at Braga, Oporto, Lamego, and Coimbra). Some of these edifices have preserved their fortress-like appearance (at Lisbon and Guarda).

The Gothic Style

South of the Mondego, art forms evolved towards the Gothic, but the sobriety and vigor of the Romanesque style so accurately suited the prevailing Portuguese temperament that Alcobaça, despite its ogival arches, is a witness to a certain characteristic restraint.

At the end of the 13th century, King Dinis, a prodigious builder, began replacing the transitional Gothic with a more typically Portuguese style, as evidenced in churches (Santa Clara-a-Velha, in Coimbra, Leça do Balio and the monastery at Odivelas), fortresses, and castles (Leiria, Estremoz, Beja). Handsome cloisters have survived from this period, at Guimarães, Coimbra, Lisbon, and Evora.

The Portuguese ogival style found its highest development at Batalha, which was influenced by English perpendicular Gothic and had grafted on to it that most original and expressive of styles, the Manueline.

The latter seems to have sprung forth spontaneously, as a kind of exaltation of the extraordinary epic of the Portuguese Discoveries. The magnificence of the Manueline style was made possible by the gold and spices that poured into the country. Exotic new worlds, either just discovered or integrated into the Christian universe, gave it its exuberant and occasionally pagan shapes. The stone, for all its rigidity, throbs with an inner dynamism, a hidden pulse, that makes the very columns contort and writhe in the Church of Jesus at Setúbal; the cables twist themselves into knots in the roof at Viseu; and the lace foams and froths in Batalha's Unfinished Chapels. Unlike the sprawling Spanish *plateresque,* Manueline art gathers itself up into medallions set against the stark simplicity of bare expanses. In the ultimate analysis, the window of Tomar's Chapter House of the Order of Christ is but a single outsized votive offering.

Art—from Renaissance to Modern

The Manueline style failed to survive beyond the lifetime of the man responsible for giving it both its name and its impetus. Almost as a reaction, João III introduced a classicism that found its expression in the Tomar cloisters. An Italian architect, Felipe Terzi, was entrusted by Philip II of Spain with all the royal projects: the coastal fortifications, the aqueduct at Vila do Conde, and the churches of São Vicente de Fora and São Roque in Lisbon (end of the 16th century).

In the early 18th century, a German, Frederic Ludwig, won the favor of King João V, the "magnificent king." Ludwig's feeling for spaciousness and generous proportions manifested itself in Mafra (1730). His Portuguese disciples had a greater sense of gracefulness. The earthquake in 1755 razed the center of Lisbon to the ground. For the rebuilding of the city, an elegant but restrained style known as "Pombaline" was introduced: the masterpiece of this period is Lisbon's Praça do Comércio (formerly the Terreiro do Paço).

The richest expression of church decoration is in the Rococo retables made of polychrome and gilded carved wood. Angels, birds, branches, shells, trophies, and pinnacles embellish the altars of churches rebuilt in the late 17th and 18th centuries, finding their way even into Romanesque and Gothic sanctuaries. The most extraordinary example of this strange and lovely art is to be found in the church of São Francisco in Oporto, where a late Gothic church has been entirely covered—pillars, arches, groined ceiling—in a plethora of superb carved and golden wood. It is fortunate that these 17th- and 18th-century additions were not removed when a passion for restoring churches and other buildings to their original state struck Portugal in the first half of this century. The great golden interior of Alcobaça was only removed around 1910, leaving that fine structure evocative but bare. However, there is still splendid Baroque and Rococo work in churches all over the country, many of which will be mentioned in their respective chapters. This golden fantasy is often allied to bright blue and white tiled panels of scriptural subjects, and strangely enough the two fantasies complement each other.

Apart from ecclesiastical art, this style did produce charming private residences (*solares, palacetes,* and *quintas*), frequently tinted in delicate shades—pinks, grays, and whites—and accented, in the Minho, with granite festoons and tiles of many hues. Landscaped gardens complete with fountains, pools, and statuary provide a setting for, or a prolongation of, these exquisite houses that can be seen both in Lisbon and in some out-of-the-way villages. The most interesting examples are found in the north, at Viana do Castelo, Vila Real, and Braga.

Until the end of the last century, Portuguese artisans and working masons built beautifully proportioned houses and little cottages by some strange inner instinct. Then, after a brief flirtation with art nouveau after World War I, examples of which can be seen all over Lisbon, the modern love of concrete took over. Even so, the acres of apartment houses outside Lisbon and other large towns are often painted in bright colors, the balconies alive with climbing geraniums, and natural stone is used for window and door frames which gives a certain dignity to the most uninspired buildings.

Sculpture and Painting

A number of Iron Age sculptures have been found in the north of the country in the course of the last hundred years. The best collection is in the Martins Sarmento Museum in Guimarães, of which the outstanding exhibit is the Colossus of Pedralva. This huge seated figure in granite with its powerful face and limbs, is one of the most remarkable prehistoric statues in Europe, yet seems to be almost unknown, even in Portugal.

Although in the pre-Romanesque portals and capitals Portuguese sculpture remained somewhat awkward and barbaric, it found its first ideal outlet in funerary monuments. The visitor to Coimbra is struck by the mannered realism in the recumbent figures of the kings and bishops on the tombs in Santa Cruz, and the original Gothic tomb of St. Isabel of Portugal in the choir of Santa Clara-a-Nova as well as the tombs in the cathedrals of Lisbon, Guarda, and Braga. These sculptures are a foretaste of the masterpiece of their kind, the tombs of Pedro and Inês at Alcobaça (circa 1367). The rich sarcophagus embellishments give full rein to the Portuguese feeling for expressive form, much more so than do the carved portals and altarpieces. The attitudes of the reclining figures—many of them are portrait-like—are stirringly eloquent: the perfect union of João I and Philippa, symbolizing also the English alliance, expresses itself in the two figures clasping each other by the hand as they lie under the high ceiling of the Founder's Chapel in Batalha.

The finest retables are the work of the French sculptors Nicholas Chantarene, Jean de Rouen, and Houdart. Their masterpieces may be seen in Coimbra, Evora, and Guarda.

An 18th-century Portuguese sculptor named Machado de Castro produced the greatest equestrian statue of his time: that of King José I, on Lisbon's Praça do Comércio. Responsible also for the impressive figures at Mafra, Machado de Castro was equally successful with miniatures: in his Nativity groups, the innumerable tiny clay figures reveal details that provide invaluable insight into the everyday life of the time (costumes, tools, utensils, accessories). His crowning achievement in this branch of art, the world's largest and finest Nativity scene, is in the Estrela Basilica in Lisbon.

In modern Portuguese sculpture, as exemplified by such craftsmen as Canto da Maia and Barata Feio, the outstanding feature is restraint, the attitude of a figure sufficing to delineate the personality of the subject—see the work of Francisco Franco (statues of Queen Leonor at Caldas da Rainha and of King Duarte at Viseu) and of Alvaro de Brée (statue of João III at Coimbra University). The work of Artur Rosa, João Cutileiro and Fernando Conduto is also of interest.

Portuguese painting came into being in the 15th century with Nuno Gonçalves. In his polyptych of São Vicente now in Lisbon's Museum of Ancient Art, this artist, obviously under Flemish influences, outshines his teachers by his use of composition, the deep brilliance of his coloring, and the amazing accuracy of his portraiture. This picture is a masterpiece that immortalizes on its panels the princes and knights, the monks and fishermen, the great names and the anonymous people of Portugal at the time of the Discoveries. *Ecce Homo,* noted for its filmed eyes, dates from the same period. Camões sang of this time, Nuno Gonçalves painted those who lived it. This was also the period of Frei Carlos of Evora, Gregorio Lopes, and Cristovão de Figueiredo.

The paintings by the Manueline artists also testify to the glory of their epoch. Caravelles sail up the Rhine on the panels of Santa Auta, and one of the Three Wise Men in the Adoration scene at Viseu is a Tupi Indian. The great Vasco (Vasco Fernandes) is harsher and more earthy. His style is distinguished by the vigor of its compositions, its expressive naturalism, plus a certain awkwardness.

The 18th century was one of decorative art: artists painted ceilings *à la* Quillard, frescos *à la* Pillement; they painted carriages, and family portraits. Living his formative years in the war-torn time of the Napoleonic invasions, Domingos Sequeira developed certain distinguishing traits of style set off by a Goyaesque bitterness.

The Victorian age saw a flowering of landscape painting, a branch of art which previous Portuguese painters had ignored. The work of José Malhoa, Miguel Angelo Lupi, who painted in the pre-Raphaelite manner, Silva Porto, Columbano, Luciano Freire and João Reis is a revelation. Their work is best seen in the José Malhoa Museum at Caldas da Rainha.

Contemporary Portuguese painting, which ranks among its pioneers such artists as Amadeu de Sousa Cardoso, who was a friend of Braque and Modigliani, and Almada Negreiros, has achieved world fame with Vieira da Silva. Other well-known painters are Noronha da Costa, Bartolomeu dos Santos, Lourdes Castro, Mário Eloy, Júlio Pomar, Paula Rego, Eduardo Nery, Francisco Smith and Menez.

Decorative Arts

Throughout the centuries, the ceramic tiles of Arabic origin known as azulejos have continued to develop. Early examples of this art have designs in relief, often geometrical motifs, as shown at Bacalhoa or in the old *Paço* in Sintra. By the 17th century the relief patterns had disappeared and been replaced by whole panels of smooth, glazed tiles with religious or secular motifs which decorated churches, palaces and private houses. In some places patterned tiles were joined together so as to look like Persian carpets. (The most beautiful tiles are in the Fronteira Palace and gardens at São Domingos de Benfica on the outskirts of Lisbon.)

The 18th century was characterized by landscapes, allegories, Biblical scenes, hunting excursions, pleasure parties (see the rare collection at the old University in Evora). In rebuilding Lisbon, polychrome tiles were used for the decoration of standard constructions and to conceal unsightly restorations. They are to be seen even covering the whole façade of a house. Emerging from the mass production of the last century, the azulejo, under the fresh impetus of such talented ceramists as Cargaleiro, Jorge Barradas, Maria Keil, Júlio Pomar, Carlos Botelho, Sá Nogueira and Querubim Lapa, has been restored to its proper place in decoration and architecture.

Wrought Gold and Tapestries

Portuguese wrought gold is outstanding in religious and other forms. The treasures in cathedrals (Evora, Viseu) and museums (Lisbon, Oporto, Coimbra) trace the development of this art from the early Romanesque crosses and chalices through to the Germanic-type vessels, including the era of Manueline splendor. The 16th-century monstrance in the Museu Nacional de Arte Antiga (Ancient Art Museum) in Lisbon, made with the first gold to reach Portugal from the Orient, is a superb example.

The Arraiolos carpets were originally wool embroideries based on Oriental rug designs, subsequently developing their own distinctive themes and colorings. They are now being produced from original designs or patterned after early models. You will see strikingly beautiful examples in all the museums.

The Portalegre tapestry studios are flourishing, and are using designs by both Portuguese (Lapa, Camarinha, Tavares) and foreign artists (Lurçat). Tapestries are used in the decoration of many public buildings and luxury hotels.

Porcelain, Pottery and Glass

The Vista Alegre porcelain works near Ílhavo were founded in 1824 by José Ferreira Pinto Basto and are still owned by the same family, many of the highly skilled craftsmen being descendants of the original workers. The porcelain is the same kind of hard type as that produced by the Berlin factory and the works still makes lovely things—not only table services but vases and ornaments in both traditional and modern styles. There are other porcelain factories in the country, but none of them approach Vista Alegre in quality.

Pottery, as has been indicated, is made all over the country and differs widely in design and color according to the clay from which it is fashioned.

Near Lisbon at Sobreiro between Mafra and Ericeira, José Franco makes original pottery pieces, as well as beautiful, simple pearl-gray plates and jugs for which the district has long been noted. Potters in the Alentejo specialize in red earthenware vessels, still modeled on traditional Roman forms, though those from Nisa are decorated with small pebbles. At Barcelos in the north they use a black clay as well as making the gaily-colored roosters for which the town is famous. Caldas da Rainha is noted for vivid green leaf plates and dishes, and these are also made in off-white. Perhaps the best known to visitors is the Olaria Pottery in the Algarve, three km. (two miles) west of Porches on the main road from Faro to Lagoa and Portimão. The Pottery was started by an Englishman, the late Patrick Swift, and specializes in high-quality hand-painted ceramics in a wide variety of both modern and traditional designs.

The Marinha Grande Glass Factory was also started by an Englishman, John Beare, in 1748, but was enlarged and developed in 1769 by William Stephens, who with his brother John left the business to the Portuguese state. The factory still produces fine table glass and decorative pieces.

PORTUGUESE CUISINE

The Western world has adopted many boringly standardized attitudes to life—jeans, jazz and junk food among them. Everywhere on the continent of Europe the hamburger reigns supreme, with Coke and, for the delectation of the British, fish and chips close behind. This omnipresence of dull, safe food has forced the adventurous traveler to acknowledge what was once one of the less vital facts of touring—that local produce, cooked according to centuries-old recipes, can provide a fascinating and real contact with the essential character of a nation. This is especially true of Portugal, where a varied and idiosyncratic cuisine reflects the nation's rich past. Meats and fish are usually marinated with wine, olive oil, garlic or herbs before being cooked—Fresh coriander in particular is used in many dishes, adding a delicious flavor.

The northern dietary tradition rests on butter and fats, but Portugal belongs to the civilization of oil *(azeite)*. Olive oil, naturally, but it is stronger and less refined than most varieties used in Spain. It may happen that olive oil does not really agree with you, and in that case, local dishes cooked in butter or corn oil *(oleo)* will always be found available.

It is readily conceded that, speaking generally, the quality of meat is indifferent but that game is excellent, and that fish, and all that the sea has to offer in the way of seafood, is superb. Vegetables are cropped early in the season, fruit is abundant, and desserts are a revelation. Fruit and vegetables are not usually imported, so one eats what is in season and freshly gathered. These considerations are intended for the fainthearted, the hesitant, and mothers of traveling families. Having said this, let us review in detail some local specialties fully deserving of the gourmet's attention.

Soups and Entrées

The mainstay of all festivities and formal occasions is soup, made of vegetables in season, boiled together and sieved with a spoonful of olive oil added at the end, or it may be *canja*. This consists of the liquid in which a chicken and the chopped liver and gizzard have been boiled. When the chicken is removed a handful of rice is thrown in. The broth of the Portuguese boiled dinner, *cozido*, in which meat, poultry, fat bacon, smoked sausage, rice and chick peas are simmered together, is a delicious and very sustaining soup. It is more a main dish than a soup, as is *açorda,* from the Alentejo, which can be likened to a kind of porridge but is based on wheat bread oiled and garlicked and offering the following alternatives: white fish (such as cod) with boiled eggs (which must be soft), and flavored with herbs such as coriander. The *açorda* is a complete repast in itself; fragrant, filling without being in the least heavy (babies—even delicate ones—are brought up on it). In Evora, you should try those offered at the *Pousada dos Loios,* which are delicious.

Very different is the true Alentejo soup, where chopped-up fat bacon is melted with a little smoked ham in a pan with two or three sliced onions; water is then added and salt and pepper to season. When the water boils, eggs are then broken in; when these are poached, a piece of bread is placed in each soup plate and the liquid poured onto it with an egg in each plate. For another Alentejo soup which requires no cooking, a good deal of garlic and fresh coriander leaves are chopped with olive oil into the bottom of a soup tureen—boiling water is then added and a few pieces of bread, and eaten at once.

The *caldo verde* from the Minho in the north is served in a bowl. Basically it consists of green cabbage shredded thinly into a clear potato broth and with slices of smoked, peppery sausages. Wholesome chunks of corn bread are eaten with it. Fish soups are also good, made by adding a little rice, onions, tomatoes, potatoes and a tablespoon of olive oil to the stock in which fish has been boiled.

The hot entrées are fine indeed: meat or fish croquettes, rissoles of seafood, stuffed pancakes or fritters. Rice *(arroz)* is equally delicious: garnished with mussels, shell fish, tunny, chicken, rabbit or simply onions, tomatoes, pimentoes or turnip tops.

Seafood

There was a time in Portugal when crayfish was served with every meal. Highly valued, it is now exported and has become scarce. Specialists in eating places still offer it today but at prices that not everyone is prepared to pay. Portuguese crayfish are so fleshy that they can be enjoyed just boiled, although some prefer them grilled or steamed *(lagosta suada),* and served with hot sauce such as will be offered on the beaches at Guincho or Peniche. Specialist restaurants display windows of seashells arranged in intriguing mosaics in Lisbon (around the Rossio) and on the far bank of the Tagus, at Cacilhas. Crabs *(santolas),* which are consumed stuffed, crayfish, prawns and shrimps *(camarões)* all entice the gourmet. Shellfish abound along the coastal regions at all times. Bringing to your lips the very taste of the waves are the astonishing *percebes,* but only of course when they are in season.

There are, however, hardly any oysters at all, and in the past they were eaten cooked. The celebrated "Portuguese" oysters, with which the oyster-beds of the Vendée were seeded, are now beginning to be offered in their natural state. Somehow neither the conveyance of these delicacies, nor their preservation in their own water has really been achieved successfully, and care should be taken to check their freshness before eating them. Oysters from the Tagus or the Sado are flat and insipid. Far more tasty are mussels *(mexilhões)* and the tiny shellfish known as *ameijoas.*

When in Algarve, you should try a *cataplana:* cockles served with sausages and ham, bringing to the table the scented fragrance of the herbs with which they are sprinkled, and cooked in an intriguing circular tin or copper utensil with a close-fitting lid, brilliant like a miniature radiant sun or moon.

Fish is available everywhere in almost confusing abundance. If you are a lover of the outdoors, you will relish grilling your own catch of mackerel in their blue spotted jackets, gray mullet or sea bream, on those little earth-enware fire-pots in which charcoal is kept aglow with a small fan woven in straw. In their humble ways, sea fishermen also have kept their own special recipes such as *caldeiradas,* a type of stew that demands an abundance of onions, fresh tomatoes, as many fish as are available, potatoes, oil and a sweetish paprika named *colorão.*

Among the many tasty fish available are sole *(linguado),* bass *(robalo),* brill *(cherne),* merou *(garoupa)* and hake *(pescada).* It is best to eat them grilled or *meuniére.* At Setúbal you should ask for red mullet *(salmonetes).* The nacrous flesh of the swordfish *(espadarte),* smelt *(carapau),* tunny steaks *(atum)* and the sea or conger eel *(safio)* are well worth going a long way to find. As for the sardine *(sardinha),* long ago it brought Portugal fame on the tables of the world. When they are fresh, try them grilled over charcoal, accompanied by a salad of tomatoes and green peppers. Another way of cooking them when they are fresh is to fillet them, roll them in oatmeal, and then fry them—it takes away some of the richness.

Do not allow the thought of cuttlefish *(chocos)* and squid *(lulas)* to intimidate you, but eat them cooked in butter with lemon, stuffed or stewed. The octopus *(polvo)* is even more impressive, and if tender, in pilaw or with tomatoes, it will confirm the general opinion that it is far superior to the best tinned crayfish. Smoked swordfish *(espadarte)* can well support comparison with smoked salmon.

High in the fish league is dried cod *(bacalhau).* The Portuguese simply love this strange dried salt fish which has to be soaked in water overnight before it is possible to cook it. It has now become expensive so few can afford to eat it often, though it is usually to be found on the menus of both simple and grand restaurants.

Every true Portuguese relishes a dish of boiled dried cod with cabbage, turnips, large onions, potatoes and a hard-boiled egg, covered in olive oil with crushed garlic and olives. But, perhaps fortunately, there are 364 other ways of dealing with this fish, some of which may be noted. First in rissoles *(pasteis de bacalhau):* when offered in taverns and snack-bars they are usually cold, and therefore less tasty than when served hot from the frying pan when they are deliciously light and melting.

Bacalhau Gomes da Sá is made by flaking the boiled fish and melting it in a deep pan with olive oil, sliced boiled potatoes, sliced onions and stoned black olives. When everything is tender the dish is served with sliced hard-boiled eggs and chopped parsley on top. It is also excellent with boiled chick peas used instead of potatoes. A lighter way of preparing this bacalhau is to add a small amount of shredded boiled cod to a couple of chopped onions melted in butter with half a dozen beaten eggs. This delicious variant of scrambled eggs should not be over-cooked.

A wealth of fresh-water fish inhabit the rivers of Portugal: lampreys *(lampreias)* and salmon *(salmao)* in the Minho, eels *(eiroz* or *anguias)* from the marshlands, the incomparable trout *(trutas)* of the Serra da Estrela or from the torrents of Madeira but now only too often from trout farms, and shad *(savel)* from the Tagus and the Douro. In the spring, in Oporto they smoke shad *(savel fumado)*, using for the process venerable oak wine barrels still gorged with the memory of brandies of long ago. It is delicious, as is the smoked eel.

One last word concerns wines: sardines and dried salt cod are consumed with red wine, contrary to all other fish dishes.

Meat, Poultry and Game

Portugal is not favored as regards grazing land, which explains the scarcity of red meat. Beef, which responds to the uncompromising name of *carne de vaca,* is seldom tender enough for the ordinary grill except in the Ribatejo, in the Azores, or understandably, in the grill rooms of the leading restaurants. Nevertheless, you will find in taverns some juicy *bifes à portugesa* with a sweet paprika and red wine sauce, served sizzling hot in an earthenware dish, and perhaps topped with a fried egg. In Madeira you may try an interesting recipe for *espetadas,* consisting of a kind of kebab of beef marinated in oil, wine and garlic, then skewered on to branches of the bay tree. This is set to roast in the fragrance of wood fires and eaten in the open. If in a hurry, you will enjoy a *prego,* a sandwich of hot beef-steak, sometimes associated with smoked ham.

The *cozido* is a boiled dish, interesting because of all that goes into it: meat, poultry, fat bacon, a diversity of sausages, rice and chick-peas. The liquid makes the soup referred to above. Veal *(vitela)* can be disappointing.

Here and there in the countryside one sees sheep *(carneiro)* eating meagerly off arid and bitter pastures. The poor fellow remains thin, with too little meat and scarcely any fat. In the country regions both sheep and goat are made to serve some purpose in the kitchen. In Beira they stew the meat at great length in a wine sauce. This is the *chanfana* of Buçaco. More tender and therefore preferable, is the kid *(cabrito)* and lamb *(borrego)*, either cooked together in a sort of spring stew such as *ensopado* or *sarapatel,* or soaked in herb juices and skewered as they eat it in Ribatejo.

But if all this talk of skinny sheep and stringy beef bodes ill for the carnivorous reader, do not despair yet, for in complete contrast, pork *(carne de porco)* is excellent and abundant. Both in the cork-oak forests of Alentejo and the rocky heaths of the north are healthy breeds of pigs. In the Alentejo they find that succulent diet of acorns and white truffles which they relish, and the aromatic shrubs of the heathlands make the meat sweet-scented and firm. The cooked meats for instance are quite special. Quite apart from the more esoteric fancies such as sugared black pudding, you must try the dried ham *(presuntos)*, smoked loin of pork rolled into a tight bolster *(paios* and *salpicoes)*, and the lean or fat meat, which form the basis of some of the best typical dishes.

In the popular taverns of Lisbon one may be served panfuls of liver with onions *(iscas)*. In Alentejo, they roast lean pork fillets with cockles over charcoal, or embers of the cork-oak. Shellfish, tasting of the sea, go admirably with the fragrant juices of the pork. Around Coimbra you must taste suckling-pig, sizzling and straight from the oven. Deliciously browned and crackling, generous helpings of pepper relieve the insipidity of the tender meat. This is a further pretext for indulging in the sparkling local wine *(Bairrada)*. In Madeira pork is occasionally perfumed with cinnamon.

The sausages differ slightly in every part of the country, but they are almost always smoked and should be eaten in stews, as a relish with rice or spaghetti, in an omelette, or sliced in a sandwich. Generally speaking, the smoked varieties are better not eaten neat as they are very rich, though delicious flambéed in brandy.

One specialty to note is smoked pigs' tongues, which are unknown outside Portugal. These should be soaked all night and then slowly boiled till tender, when they make an unusual dish that can be eaten either hot or cold. Other pig products are trotters stewed with dried beans, and liver or kidneys.

Barbecues *(churrascos)*, particularly chicken barbecues, are the "in" thing. African pepper, known as *piripiri,* can be used excessively on such occasions—perhaps because it stimulates the thirst and helps to get the party going with an alcoholic swing. You will be better off when the chicken has been cooked without the gunpowder. The *dobrada à moda do Porto* consisted originally of tripe and beans; it dates back to the days when the Infante Dom Henrique, preparing his father's expedition against Ceuta, slaughtered and salted all available cattle in the area, and left the unfortunate inhabitants only the offal and tripe. Today, the recipe is infinitely more sophisticated, and includes chicken, sausages, carrots, and tomatoes; it is very tasty indeed. You should keep an eye open for turkey *(peru)*. In Portugal the bird is fed with bread soaked in brandy before it is killed, which not only makes the bird dizzy but is supposed to improve the flavor and make it tender. When the bird is ready for cooking, it is rubbed with coarse salt and lemon and stuffed with a mixture of the giblets, ground veal, pork, fat bacon, onion, bread crumbs, stoned olives and eggs, sautéed in lard.

In the regions where game is to be found, there are as many recipes as there are cooks to deal with the harvest of partridges *(perdizes)*, pigeons *(borrachos)*, quail *(codornizes)*, and snipe *(galinholas)*.

Almost every dish in Portugal is accompanied by either rice or fried potatoes, or both. The best-known salads are lettuce *(alface)*, which is always rather green, watercress *(agrioes)* and tomato and pimento *(tomate e pimento)*. *Chicarolas,* a type of chicory, are excellent when obtainable.

Cheeses

We have noted the scarcity of grazing land generally. However, good dairy produce can be found in the Azores because of its lush pastures, and also in the low-lying area in the neighborhood of Aveiro. Butter and matured cheeses from the islands are excellent, in the Danish tradition. Distinct from these, Portugal has also some genuine marvels for those with a nose for the good things of life. These are seasonal cheeses which should be eaten in winter and spring, like the *queijo da Serra,* which sheds generous tears of cream in the grocers' windows, and is made of ewes' milk, kneaded by hand and matured in cool cellars.

Rather more robust is the *queijo d'Azeitao,* also made with ewes' milk, or the *Serpa,* which is drier. As its name indicates, the *cabreiro* displays all the power of the goat from whose milk it is extracted. White or cottage cheese are occasionally eaten salted *(queijinhos de Tomar).* When consumed fresh, the *requeijao* or the *queijinho fresco* are silky and feathery and quite exquisite, particularly when eaten moist as they come from their little basket or tin molds. A portion of fresh cheese is often put on your table in restaurants for you to nibble at between courses.

Sweets and Desserts

Portugal has a sweet tooth. Each and every Portuguese lady jealously hides her book of original recipes, but the one universal dessert is the flan pudding (or *crème caramel*) that appears on the menu of every restaurant.

In truth the great variety of Portuguese sweets is due mostly to their intricate presentation, and to a lesser degree to imperceptible differences in flavor which the casual consumer cannot detect. The basis is egg yolk baked in sugar. In Aveiro, *ovos moles* come to you in amusing little barrels. In Caldas, *trouxas d'ovos* are soaked in thick syrup. In Abrantes, *palhas* are a golden marvel. Fifty and more specialties are just variations on a single theme. Marvelous things, yet somewhat heavier, are concocted if almonds are added to the stock recipes: to that order belong the *morgado* and the *Dom Rodrigo* from Algarve, and a host of elaborations whose names bear clerical associations; *barrigas de freiras* (nuns' "tummies") or *toucinho do ceú* (bacon from heaven). The marzipans of Alentejo and Algarve are wrought in perfect imitation of every conceivable object: animal, vegetable or mineral, decorative and exquisite. In Algarve, fantasy dictates patterns with dates and figs, chessboard and mosaics, a hen and her brood of chicks, longhaired dogs, or a turkey strutting with tail spread.

One of the glories of the ancient convents used to be quince cheese (*marmelada,* from which our word marmalade is derived), perfumed with vanilla, lemon and bergamot, the most famous being that of Odivelas. *Pasteis de Nata* are small tarts which in Belém are made with custard and cinnamon, or with cheese *(queijadas)* at Sintra and Funchal. In Torres Vedras they are filled with beans. The traditional dessert for weddings is rice pudding *(arroz doce),* made with custard and adorned with patterns traced in cinnamon.

Fruits? Fundão is famous for pears, Setúbal for oranges, Elvas for plums, Algarve for figs and almonds. Early strawberries and avocado pears are now being grown commercially in the Algarve. The small prickly red balls of fruit from the *medronha* or strawberry tree make a delicious liqueur. The fruit alone is said to be intoxicating. Apricots, large yellow peaches and nectarines *(péssegos carecas)* are the specialty of the rich lands around Alcobaça where they are also preserved and bottled.

Crystalized fruit is now expensive, but if you are passing through Elvas be sure to pick up a box of plums, they make an excellent present. Local specialties include, at Setúbal, orange *fondants* and at Coimbra, large soft *dragées* which are a feature at Easter-time. Portugal owes to its temperate climate a profusion of fresh fruit: melons of many sizes and hues, from the golden cantaloupe, dripping sugar, and the big red-fleshed water melons *(melancias)* with large black seeds, to green honeydew, which is faintly peppery in taste. There are grapes, naturally, in bewildering abundance, and pineapples from the Azores, as well as sweet oranges. There are also fresh loquats or medlars *(nesperas)*. Pride of place, if only for exotic appeal, must go to the produce of the Islands, which will be to many a succulent revelation: custard apples *(anonas)* from Madeira, the flesh of which is creamy and fragrant, and the *maracujá* or passionfruit. To these should be added the better-known mangoes, avocados, and guava.

Vegetables are eaten in their season, broad beans being particularly good when simmered with coriander. Wild asparagus with its slightly bitter taste goes well with roast chicken and can be picked up on any deserted ground in the early spring.

PORTUGUESE WINE

With the exception of those classic Kings of Wines, Port and Madeira, the wines that Portugal produces are mainly honest and straightforward, unaccompanied by the snobbish mystique that shrouds French vintages. This is a country where the ordinary visitor who likes wine can enjoy an endless procession of delicious experiments for little more than the cost of a good beer. It is also possible to find wines of some age that in other countries would be very expensive, but can be enjoyed here at a very moderate cost.

Not that the history of wine in Portugal is shorter or less distinguished than the history of wine in other Continental countries. It stretches back beyond the Romans to the Phoenicians, flourished still under the teetotal Moslems, and went through a checkered time after the Moors were expelled. One of the mainstays of the wine trade's prosperity in Portugal—especially where Port was concerned—was the firm link with Britain. The trade between the two countries predates the 1386 Treaty of Windsor possibly by two centuries. After a long period of generally spasmodic development, with some regions flourishing while others, such as the Algarve, almost ceased production, the situation was taken in hand by Pombal—one of the many facets of Portuguese life that he tried to improve by diktat. In 1756 he put into operation a national plan for "demarcated" regions, geographically delineating growing areas and controlling their output and marketing, with the Port region the first to be demarcated.

Demarcation, and the attendant control of quality, really took off in the first years of this century, and there are now ten regions officially demarcated—the Algarve, Moscatel de Setúbal, Bucelas, Carcavelos, Colares, Bairrada, Dão, Douro, Vinho Verdes, and the island of Madeira.

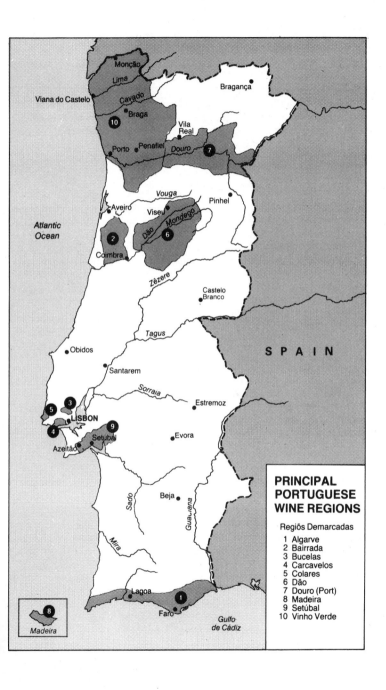

Monção
Lima
Cavado
Braga
Bragança
Viana do Castelo
10
Vila Real
Porto Penafiel Douro 7
Vouga
Aveiro Pinhel
Viseu
Atlantic Ocean
Dão Mondego 6
2
Coimbra
Zêzere
Castelo Branco
Tagus
Obidos
Santarem
SPAIN
Sorraia
Estremoz
5 3
LISBON
4 9
Azeitão Setúbal
Evora
Sado
Beja
Guadiana
Mira
Lagoa
1
Faro
Gulfo de Cádiz
8
Madeira

PRINCIPAL PORTUGUESE WINE REGIONS

Regiõs Demarcadas

1 Algarve
2 Bairrada
3 Bucelas
4 Carcavelos
5 Colares
6 Dão
7 Douro (Port)
8 Madeira
9 Setúbal
10 Vinho Verde

The official body that looks after wine production is the Junta Nacional do Vinho (J.N.V.), based in Lisbon. It controls all the facets of viniculture and of marketing, runs competitions, promotes cooperatives (important in the new political climate of the country), and empowers growers to use a seal of approval *(selo de origem)*, rather like the French *appelation d'origine*, which acts as a protection for the public. There are several areas which are undemarcated still, such as those around Evora, but which nonetheless produce excellent wines.

It is still too early to judge how the convoluted regulations on wine that the E.E.C. try to operate will affect Spain and Portugal, who are very recent recruits to the organization, but, as both countries represent a threat to the entrenched interests of the older members, especially France, it is certain that they will have a considerable impact in the long run.

The Algarve and the Alentejo

Starting in the south, and working our way up-country, we will begin with a quick look at the wines produced in the southernmost demarcated region, the Algarve. The vast proportion of tourism to Portugal is down here, among the almond blossoms, concrete hotels, and wide sandy beaches. Most of the Algarve's wine is produced in a comparatively narrow strip of land stretching between the mountains and the sea. Algarve wine is largely red, with a tiny proportion of white, and is often not unlike a good table wine, a carafe type. Among the better makes is *Lagoa*.

Higher up-country lies the Alentejo, usually known to visitors—at least in its southern reaches—simply as a wide tract of land to get across as quickly as possible when heading for the Algarve beaches. But this view isn't really fair to the province, which can be quite lovely at certain times of year, especially in spring. The Alentejo vineyards, not yet demarcated, are almost all in the top part of the province, around Evora and over towards the Spanish border. The wines they produce even have a Spanish look and taste to them—*Redondo, Borba* (with its lovely dark color and slightly metallic flavor), *Beja,* and *Vidigueira.* They are all worth seeking out, the reds rich in color, the whites tending to be pale, with a distinct tang. All are very strong in alcohol content, so drink carefully.

The Regions Around Lisbon

There are four demarcated regions within easy reach of Lisbon—Moscatel de Setúbal, Bucelas, Carcavelos, and Colares.

The Setúbal Peninsula lies below Lisbon, across the Tagus, and is now easily reached by a through highway. It is worth exploring for many reasons, not least to discover the peace of the wooded and rocky Serra d'Arrábida. The wines produced here are well known abroad, mainly through the 150-year efforts of the House of Fonseca, based on Azeitão in the heart of the peninsula. The Moscatel which Fonseca produces, together with the small vinegrowers who make up the local cooperative in Palmela—a few miles east of Azeitão and boasting a superb pousada—is best known as a fortified dessert wine, aged and with a mouthwatering taste of honey. If you manage to find some that is, say, 25 years old, then you will find it has a licorice color, and enjoy its sweet scent and taste. Fonseca and the cooperative produce many other wines as well as the Moscatel—fine reds (notably one called *Periquita,* or "little parrot"); rosés, of which *Lancers* and *Faisca* are much exported; and some ordinary whites, as distinct from the dessert ones, though nothing like as many as are produced elsewhere in the country.

Although Fonseca has a very old winery in Azeitão itself, there is a fascinating modern installation on the eastern edge of the little town. It is a series of great white tanks, looking for all the world like a collection of half-buried flying saucers.

The Bucelas region is situated around 30 km. (19 miles) north of the capital, in the valley of the River Trancão. Though wine from here has a considerable history, and was very popular with the British soldiers under Wellington in the Peninsular War, this is quite a small demarcated region, and all the wine it produces appears under the *Caves Velhas* label. The Bucelas wine is usually straw colored, with a distinctively full nose and a fruity taste, which can sometimes verge on the citrus. It makes an extremely good companion for the lighter kind of white meats, veal and poultry, and is especially appropriate with fish.

Carcavelos consists of just one smallish vineyard, the Quinta do Barão, sandwiched between Lisbon and Estoril along a stretch of overdeveloped and popular coastline. This is not an easy wine to find, the yearly output being quite small, but if you are interested in wines with a history, it would be worth searching out for your collection. Carcavelos is another fortified dessert wine, topaz colored, with a nutty aroma and a slightly almond taste, mostly drunk as an aperitif.

The last of the four demarcated regions around Lisbon is Colares, on the westernmost tip of Portugal, beyond Sintra. It is a fairly hostile place for vine growing, with sandy soil and exposed to the Atlantic winds. Like Carcavelos, the spread of Lisbon's commuter belt has squeezed this region which is a pity, as it has a long and distinguished history of wine production, and still yields some very individual vintages, especially red. This is a wine that definitely improves with age, of a full ruby color, an aromatic nose, and an aftertaste which is likened to blackcurrants. It can be a little astringent when young, so it is always wise to try to find one of the older years. One label to seek out might be *Colares Chita.* The Colares whites are straw colored, slightly nutty in taste, and—like the reds—improve with age. They should be drunk well chilled.

Bairrada and Dão

Higher up the Atlantic coast, and not far south of Oporto, is the region of Bairrada. It is not that long ago—1979—that Bairrada was demarcated, though, on the quality of its output, it probably should have been long before. This is a region made up mainly of smallholdings, gathered into six cooperatives. Taken all together, they turn out a fairly large quantity of wine. As there are several places of interest to the visitor—Coimbra, Conimbriga, Aveiro, and the Forest of Buçaco with its fantasy hotel—it may well be that you will easily come across the Bairrada wines. The reds are of an intense color, with a delicious nose, and a fruity, rich and lasting taste. They mellow with age, and go very well with stronger dishes, such as game, roasts, and the more pungent cheeses. There are not too many whites in this region, and most of them are slightly sparkling *(espumantes),* made often by the champagne method, though of course they cannot be called that, as the French champagne area has fought several legal battles to protect the name. Their characteristics mirror the reds, in having a slightly darkish straw color, with a heavy, rather spicy nose. They go well with fish, pasta and pâtés. One of the biggest names in the region, and one which has been largely exported, is *Aliança,* though several others such as *São Domingos,* and *Frei João* are worth tracking down. The hotel at Buçaco has its own wines, in an extensive cellar, and they add a delicious dimension to a visit to that exceptional place.

The Dão demarcated region—pronounced something like "down" with an adenoidal twang—is also a name quite well known outside Portugal. This region is just south of the Douro, in the mountainous heart of northern Portugal, crossed by the valleys of the Rivers Dão, Mondego and Alva. Because of its terrain, the climate is very capricious here, cold, wet winters, scorchingly hot summers. Unlike the sandy or clay soils to the south, the terrain is made up of granite and schist, a rock which shatters easily, with the resultant changes in the kind of grapes that are cultivated. A very high proportion of wine here is red, matured—they are known as *vinhos maduros*—in oak casks for at least 18 months before being bottled. When they are fully mature, they have an attractively dark reddish-brown color, almost the hue of garnets, a "complex" nose, and a lasting velvety taste. They are best drunk at room temperature after being allowed to breathe well, and go excellently with the favorite roasts of Portugal, lamb and pork. Some of the best names to look for are *São Domingos, Terras Altas,* and *Porta dos Cavaleiros,* or any of the labels where the word Dão precedes the name of the supplier—*Dão Aliança, Dão Caves Velhas, Dão Serra,* or *Dão Fundação.* The Dão whites are less common. They spend shorter times maturing in casks, though still six months or more, have the color of light straw, a full nose, and a dry, earthy flavor. The white *Grão Vasco* is certainly one to try, or *Meia Encosta.*

Douro and Port

The secret of Port is found, first of all in the nature of the arid, volcanic soil and the hothouse temperature of the Douro valley. Some 800 years ago, when the father of Afonso Henriques took possession of his new domain, between Douro and Minho, he planted a stock brought from Burgundy. The vine, like Count Henri, adjusted itself to the alien soil. "Eating lava and drinking sunshine," the Burgundy vines stretched, little by little, to the river's edge. They fought a bitter fight, strangling in ravines, wandering in fits and starts, to force their roots through schistous soil. Nothing but the vine could survive in this torrid pass. With tireless obstinacy, the men of the Douro broke up slate, built terraces with stone-retaining walls, struggled against drought and phylloxera, and made the lost valley the most prosperous in Portugal.

It comes alive during the grape gathering, which lasts for several weeks, since the grapes ripen according to exposure and altitude. In the vineyards sited at lower levels, the gathering is often finished long before the higher plantations are ripe, for cold winds blow down from the Serra do Marão. The region, usually drowsy—the population is scattered because of water shortage—suddenly springs into activity at the time of picking. Workers hurry in from neighboring provinces. From dawn until dusk girls are busy filling baskets, which the men carry on their backs, supporting as much as 150 pounds with the aid of a leather band looped over their foreheads. They descend in long files, towards the *lagares* at the foot of the slopes, pile the fruit in these enormous vessels, ready for treading. Over 40 varieties of grape go into the making of Port, creating the wide diversity of taste that the finished wines can have. The harvesters gather about the vats before the *must* has begun to ferment; the atmosphere is steamy, the feverish excitement of new wine induces singing and dancing. In the spring the young wine goes down by road to the lodges in Vila Nova de Gaia. Since the building of a dam across the river the age-old transportation of the wine by *rabelos,* those strange boats of Douro that look somewhat like ancient Phoenician craft, has ceased.

Port, born as it is of a soil rich in lava, is divided into two great families—vintage and blended. When a year is outstanding—as in 1945, '47, '48, '55, '58, '63, '70, '75, '77, '80 and '83—the wine is unblended and, after reinforcement and bottling, left to mature. These are the vintage wines, which will take upwards of 20 years to mature; the old bottles, dusty with cobwebs, are brought up from the cellar for weddings and christenings, and must be decanted before drinking.

By far the greater quantity of Port, though, even of good quality, is made of a carefully studied blend of new wine with old vintages, thereby obtaining a wide range of taste. For a long time, when England was the biggest market for Port, the first choice was given to full-bodied tawnies; these were served at the end of dinner, with cheese, or an apple and walnuts. However, there is a lot to be said for the white Ports, either sweet as an after-dinner drink, or dry, as an aperitif with ice and a twist of lemon.

The visitor to Oporto should definitely visit one of the Lodges to learn more about Port, taste it and, maybe, buy a bottle of one of the vintages that takes your fancy. It is quite an experience for anyone interested in wine to see these huge old cellars, and find out some of the long, fascinating history that Port has gathered, like the cobwebs, over the centuries. Language will be no problem, as there has been an alliance for more than 200 years between the English and Portuguese in the Port trade, and many of the families are totally bilingual.

Of course, not all the wine produced in the Douro demarcated region is Port. The reds here are of a deep ruby color, extremely fruity, and with a rounded taste. They go well with richer foods, variety meats, casseroles, and stews—anything that tends to be well flavored with herbs. The whites are dry, by and large, a pleasant pale yellow color, with a "full" nose. They go well with salads, hors d'oeuvres, and chicken dishes. Look for *Mesão Frio, San Marco, Quinta da Cotto,* and *Santa Marta.*

Vinho Verde

This is the largest demarcated region in the country, divided into six sub-regions: Monção, Lima, Amarante, Basto, Braga, and Penafiel. The area lies inland from the Atlantic coast, threaded by a sequence of westward-flowing rivers, and enjoying a fairly mild climate, with Portugal's highest rainfall.

Like *retsina* in Greece, vinho verde has come to mean Portuguese wine to many people. The name simply means "green wine," which refers to its delightful youth (as in Cleopatra's "salad days") and not to its color. For anyone who enjoys wine purely as a refreshing, mildly intoxicating beverage, a kind of celestial 7-Up, vinho verde is unquestionably *the* drink—gently sparkling (what the experts call *pétillant*), with a delicate fruity flavor, it embodies the coolness and fragrance of summer gardens. Vinho verde goes especially well with fish, or any kind of seafood. The reds are important to the region, but will mostly be found on their home ground, they don't travel much. They also are refreshingly thirst-quenching, sharp rather than heavy, but with a vermilion-to-purple color. Naturally, they go ideally with almost any meat dish. Try for *Alvarinho,* and *Quinta de São Claudio.*

The vineyards are particularly noticeable in the Vinho Verde district, as this is an area where they are frequently terraced, climbing up the hill-sides away from the rivers, like agricultural fortifications. Also, in places, they actually arch over the roads, and often march alongside as you drive, the vines held high on colonnaded rows of pillars, reaching up to the sun. The grapes hang so high that they ripen in direct sunlight, without any rising heat from the ground.

Madeira

Like Port, Madeira—our last demarcated region—deserves a chapter all to itself. This is a volcanic island, rising up to the misty retreat of Curral das Freiras, huddled in the old crater. The soil is clearly volcanic, and the beaches, such as they are, black. The climate here is temperate, but can be humid in summer, and provides exactly the conditions in which vines can thrive although seldom seen below 300 feet above sea level, that warmer zone being taken up by bananas and sugar cane production.

The history of viniculture on Madeira is almost as long as the history of man on the island, and that started in 1419. Like Port, Madeira—the wine and its preparation—is a way of life, and a way of life in which Portuguese and British families are bound together. When Charles II married Catherine of Bragança in 1662 he, perhaps foolishly, declined to accept the island as part of her dowry.

Again like Port, the modern wine has changed a great deal from the traditional drink which was much favored by George Washington, among many other famous people. The modern light, dry versions have become popular as the public's tastes have altered. Madeira is a fortified wine, and most often blended, too. The main styles are: *Bual* and *Malmsey,* the sweeter, heavier ones, which make excellent dessert wines; *Verdelho,* not so sweet, though still a little, and useful as a light between-times drink, say as an alternative to sherry; lastly, *Sercial,* dry and light, which makes an excellent aperitif. None of these, of course, is the kind of wine you are likely to drink as accompaniment to the main course of a meal, but they are all attractive occasional wines and, when they are really aged as they often are, can provide the dedicated drinker with a rare experience.

The labels to look for—and they date back in some cases for a couple of centuries—include *Blandy, Cossart Gordon, Rutherford and Miles, Lea-cock,* and *Miles and Luis Gomes* (you see what we mean about British and Portuguese families). A visit to a wine lodge in Funchal is an educational and delectable way of passing a couple of hours during your vacation.

Portuguese Wine Words

Adamado	Medium Sweet
Adega	Wine vaults
Adega Cooperativa	Wine Cooperative
Aguardente	Brandy
Branco	White
Bruto	Extra dry (for sparkling wines)
Caves	Wine cellars
Colheita	Grape harvest (thus a vintage, e.g. Colh. 1980)
Doce	Sweet
Espumante	Sparkling wine
Garrafeira (or Reserva)	Fine and mature wine. Special vintage
Generoso	An aperitif or dessert wine, highly alcoholic
Meio Seco	Medium dry
Região Demarcada	Demarcated Region (see text for explanation)
Rosado	Rosé
Seco	Dry
Tinto	Red
Velho	Old
Vinho da Mesa	Table wine
Vinho da Casa	House wine

ENGLISH-PORTUGUESE VOCABULARY

If you have a reading knowledge of Spanish and/or French, you will find Portuguese easy to read. However, Portuguese pronunciation can be somewhat tricky. Despite obvious similarities in Spanish and Portuguese spelling and syntax, the Portuguese sounds are a far cry—almost literally so—from their ostensible Spanish equivalents. Some of the main peculiarities of Portuguese phonetics are the following.

Nasalized vowels: if you have some idea of French pronunciation, these shouldn't give you too much trouble. The closest approach is that of the French *accent du Midi,* as spoken by people in Marseille and in the Provence area, or perhaps an American Midwest twang will help. Try pronouncing *"an," "am," "en," "em," "in," "om," "un,"* etc., with a sustained *"ng"* sound (e.g. *"bom"-"bong,"* etc.).

Another aspect of Portuguese phonetics is the vowels and diphthongs written with the tilde: *ã, ão, ães.* The Portuguese word for *"wool," "lã,"* sounds roughly like the French word *"lin,"* with the *"–in"* resembling the *"an"* in the English word *"any,"* but nasalized. The suffix *"–tion"* on such English words as "information" becomes in Portuguese spelling *"ção,"* pronounced *"-sa-on,"* with the *"-on"* nasalized: *"Informação,"* for example. These words form their plurals by changing the suffix to *ções,* which sounds like *"-son-ech"* (the *"ch"* here resembling a cross between the English *"sh"* and the German *"ch"*: hence *"informaçoes"*).

The cedilla occurring under the *"c"* serves exactly the same purpose as in French: it transforms the *"c"* into an *"ss"* sound in front of the three so-called "hard" vowels ("a," "o," and "u"): e.g. *graça, Açores, açúcar.* The letter "c" occurring without a cedilla in front of these three vowels automatically has the sound of "k": pico, mercado, curto. The letter "c" followed by "e" or "i" is always "ss," and hence needs no cedilla: nacional, Graciosa, Terceira.

The letter "j" sounds like the "s" in the English word "pleasure." So does "g" except when the latter is followed by one of the "hard" vowels: hence, generoso, gigantesco, Jerónimo, azulejos, Jorge, etc.

The spelling *"nh"* is rendered like the *"ny"* in *"canyon"*: cf. *"senhora."*

The spelling *"lh"* is somewhere in between the *"l"* and the *"y"* sounds in *"million"*: cf. *"Batalha."*

In the matter of syllabic stress, Portuguese obeys the two basic Spanish principles: 1) in words ending in a vowel, or in "n" or "s" the tonic accent falls on the next-to-the-last syllable: fado, mercado, azulejos; 2) in words ending in consonants other than "n" or "s," the stress falls on the last syllable: *favor, nacional.* Words in which the syllabic stress does not conform to the two above rules must be written with an acute accent to indicate the proper pronunciation: sábado, república, politécnico.

It is the "hushed," or unvoiced, vowels and consonants that make spoken Portuguese so elliptical and so complicated to follow for the untrained ear. You will find the intonations of Portuguese speech and the rise and fall of Portuguese voices quite fascinating.

VOCABULARY

BASICS

yes	sim
no	não
please	por favor
thank you	obrigado
thank you very much	muito obrigado
excuse me, sorry	com licença, desculpe
I'm sorry	desculpe-me
Good morning or good day	Bom dia
Good afternoon	Boa tarde
Good evening or good night	Boa noite
Goodbye	Adeus

NUMBERS

1	um, uma	18	dezoito	
2	dois	19	dezanove	
3	três	20	vinte	
4	quatro	21	vinte e um	
5	cinco	22	vinte e dois	
6	seis	30	trinta	
7	sete	40	quarenta	
8	oito	50	cinquenta	
9	nove	60	sessenta	
10	dez	70	setenta	
11	onze	80	oitenta	
12	doze	90	noventa	
13	treze	100	cem	
14	catorze	110	cento e dez	
15	quinze	200	duzentos	
16	dezaseis	1,000	mil	
17	dezasete	1,500	mil e quinhentos	

DAYS OF THE WEEK

Monday	Segunda-feira
Tuesday	Terça-feira
Wednesday	Quarta-feira
Thursday	Quinta-feira
Friday	Sexta-feira
Saturday	Sábado
Sunday	Domingo

MONTHS

January	Janeiro	July	Julho
February	Fevereiro	August	Agosto
March	Março	September	Setembro
April	Abril	October	Outubro
May	Maio	November	Novembro
June	Junho	December	Dezembro

COLORS

Red	Vermelho
Blue	Azul
Black	Preto
White	Branco
Green	Verde
Gray	Cinzento
Yellow	Amarelo
Orange	Cor de laranja
Brown	Castanho

USEFUL PHRASES

The most important phrase to know (one that may make it unnecessary to know any others) is: "Do you speak English?"—in Portuguese, *Fala inglês?* If the answer is *Nao,* then you may have recourse to the list below.

How are you?	Como está?
How do you say in Portuguese?	Como se diz em Português?
Tourist Office	Turismo
Fine	Optimo
Very good	Muito bem (muito bom)
It's all right	Está bem
Good luck	Felicidades (boa sorte)
Hello	Olá
Come back soon	Até breve
Where is the hotel?	Onde é o hotel?
How much does this cost?	Quanto custa?
How do you feel?	Como se sente?
How goes it?	Que tal?
Pleased to meet you	Muito prazer em o (a) conhecer
The pleasure is mine	O prazer é meu

I have the pleasure of introducing Mr. . . .	Tenho o prazer de lhe apresentar o senhor. . . .
I like it very much	Gosto muito
I don't like it	Não gosto
Many thanks	Muito obrigado
Don't mention it	De nada
Pardon me	Desculpe-me (Perdão)
Are you ready?	Está pronto?
I am ready	Estou pronto
Welcome	Seja benvindo
I am very sorry	Desculpe (Lastimo muito)
What time is it?	Que horas são?
I am glad to see you	Muito prazer em o (a) ver
I don't understand	Não entendo
Please speak slowly	Fale lentamente por favor
I understand (or) It is clear	Compreendo (or) Está claro
Whenever you please	Quando quizer
Please wait	Faça favor de esperar
I will be a little late	Chegarei um pouco atrasado
I don't know	Não sei
Is this seat free?	Está vago este lugar?
Would you please direct me to . . . ?	Por favor indique-me . . . ?
Where is the station, museum . . . ?	Onde é a estação, museum . . . ?
I am American, British	Eu sou Americano, Inglês
It's very kind of you	É muito amavel
Please sit down	Por favor sente-se

EVERYDAY NEEDS

cigar, cigarette	charuto, cigarro
matches	fosforos
dictionary	dicionário
key	chave
razor blades	laminas de barbear
shaving cream	creme de barbear
soap	sabonete
city plan	mapa da cidade
road map	mapa das estradas
country map	mapa do país
newspaper	jornal
magazine	revista
telephone	telefone
telegram	telegrama
envelopes	envelopes
writing paper	papel de carta
airmail writing paper	papel de carta de avião
post card	postal
stamps	selos

SERVICES AND STORES

bakery	padaria
bookshop	livraria
butcher's	talho
delicatessen	charcutaria
dry cleaner's	limpeza a seco
grocery	mercearia
hairdresser, barber	cabeleireiro, barbeiro
laundry	lavandaria
shoemaker	sapateiro
stationery store	papelaria
supermarket	supermercado
toilet	casa de banho

EMERGENCIES

ill, sick	doente
I am ill	estou doente
My wife/husband/child is ill	Minha mulher/marido/criança está doente
doctor	doutor/medico
nurse	enfermeira/o
prescription	receita
pharmacist/chemist	farmacia
Please fetch/call a doctor	Por favor, chame o doutor/medico
accident	acidente
road accident	acidente na estrada
Where is the nearest hospital?	Onde é o hospital mais proximo?
Where is the American/British Hospital?	Onde é o Hospital Americano/Britanico?
dentist	dentista
X-ray	Raios-X

PHARMACIST'S

pain-killer	analgésico
gauze pads	compressas de gaze
bandage	ligadura
bandaid	pensos rápidos
scissors	tesoura
hot-water bottle	saco de água quente
sanitary pads	pensos higiénicos
tampons	tampões
ointment for bites/stings	pomada para picadas
coughdrops	pastilhas para a tosse
cough mixture	xarope para a tosse
laxative	laxativo
thermometer	termómetro

TRAVELING

plane	avião
hovercraft	hovercrafte
train	comboio
boat	barco
taxi	taxi
car	carro/automovel
bus	autocarro
seat	assento/lugar
reservation	reserva
smoking/non-smoking compartment	compartimento para fumadores/não fumadores
rail station	estação caminho de ferro
subway station	estação do Metropolitano
airport	aéroporto
harbor	estação marítima
town terminal	estação/terminal
shuttle bus/train	autocarro/comboio com ligação constante
sleeper	cama
couchette	beliche
porter	bagageiro
baggage/luggage	bagagem
baggage trolley	carrinho de bagagem
single ticket	bilhete de ida
return ticket	bilhete de ida e volta
first class	primeira classe
second class	segunda classe
When does the train leave?	A que horas sai o comboio?
What time does the train arrive at . . . ?	A que horas chega o comboio a . . . ?
When does the first/last train leave?	Quando parte o primeiro/ ultimo comboio?

HOTELS

room	quarto
bed	cama
bathroom	casa de banho
bathtub	banheira
shower	duche
toilet/Men/Women	toilete/Homens/Senhores
toilet paper	papel higiénico
pillow	almofada
blanket	cobertor
chambermaid	criada/empregada de quarto
breakfast	pequeno almoço
lunch	almoço
dinner	jantar

Do you have a single/double/ twin-bedded room?	Tem um quarto individual/ duplo/com duas camas?
I'd like a quiet room	Eu gostava de um quarto sossegado
I'd like some pillows/blankets	Gostava de mais almofadas/ cobertores
What time is breakfast?	A que horas é o pequeno almoço?
Is it served in the room?	É servido no quarto?
Come in!	Entre!
Are there any messages for me?	Há algum recado para mim?
Would you please call me a taxi?	Por favor chama-me um taxi?
Please take our bags to our room	Por favor leve as nossas malas para o nosso quarto

RESTAURANTS

menu	carta
fixed-price menu	preço fixo
wine list	carta de vinhos
house wine	vinho da casa
waiter	criado/empregado
Waiter!	Faz favor!
bill/check	conta

ON THE MENU

Starters

mixed hors d'oeuvre	acepipes variados
melon	melão
pâté	pasta de fígado
soup	sopa
a rougher version of pâté	terrine
smoked ham	presunto
smoked fish	peixe fumado

Meats

lamb	borrego	mutton	carneiro
steak	bife	pork	porco
beef	carne de vaca	roast beef	carne assada
kebab	espetada	sausage	salsichas
pork cold cuts	carnes frias de porco	salami	salame
		veal	vitela
fillet steak	bife de lombo	brains	miolos
chop	costeleta	liver	fígado
rib steak	entrecosto	tongue	lingua
leg of lamb	perna de borrego	kidney	rim
ham	fiambre	sweetbreads	moleijas
bacon	bacon/toucinho fumado	tripe	dobrada

Poultry and Game

duck	pato	boiling fowl	galinha para
duckling	pato novo	cozer	
pheasant	faisão	chicken	galinha
wild boar	javali	spring chicken	frango
goose	gançо	turkey	perú
partridge	perdiz		
guinea hen/fowl	galinha da guiné		

Fish

eel	enguia	whiting	pescada
cod	bacalhau	perch	perca
sea bream	pargo	salmon	salmão
monkfish	peixe espada	trout	truta
sea bass	robalo	salmon trout	truta salmonada
mackerel	cavala		

Shellfish

prawn	gamba	lobster	lavagante
scallop	vieira/salmeira	crayfish	lagostim
shrimp	camarão	mussel	mexilhão
crawfish	lagosta	sea urchin	ouriço do mar
mixed shellfish	mista de mariscos	clam	ameijoas

Vegetables

globe artichoke	alcachofra/	zucchini	courgette
asparagus	espargos	(courgette)	
eggplant	beringela	watercress	agrião
carrot	cenoura	chicory	chicoria
mushroom	cogumelo	spinach	espinafres
cabbage	couve	broad bean	favas
sauerkraut	choucroute	kidney bean	feijão verde
cauliflower	couve flor	(green)	
white haricot		leek	alho Frances
bean	feijão manteiga	green/red	pimento verde/
French bean	feijão verde redondo	pepper	vermelho
		rice	arroz
lentil	lentilha	lettuce	alface
turnip	nabo	tomato	tomate
onion	cebola	Jerusalem	alcachofra/
potato	batata	artichoke	topinambo
pea	ervilha		

Fruit

pineapple	ananaz	melon	melão
blackcurrant	groselha preta	peach	pessego

cherry	cereja	nectarine	pessegos carecas/
lemon	limão		nectarinas
strawberry	morango	pear	pera
raspberry	framboesa	apple	maçã
blackberry	amora	apricot	aplerce
orange	laranja	plum	ameixa
grapefruit	toranja	greengage	rainha claudia
water melon	melancia	prune	ameixa seca

Desserts

fritter	filhó/sonho	fruit salad	salada de fruta
caramel custard	pudim de	water ice	sorvete
	caramelo	pie/tart/flan	tarte/flam
cake	bolo	with whipped	com natas
ice cream	gelado	cream	
chocolate	mousse de	assorted	pastelaria
mousse	chocolate	pastry	

Sauces etc.

mayonnaise	maionaise	fried, sautéed	salteado 'com
with oil and	com azeite e		manteiga
vinegar	vinagre		
dressing		lightly roasted	levemente assado
braised, fried	frito	roast	assado
smoked	fumado	rare	mal passado
browned under	gratinado com	medium (steak)	normal
grill with	queijo	well-done	bem passado
grated cheese		braised on	grelhado na
curried	com caril	charcoal	braza

Index

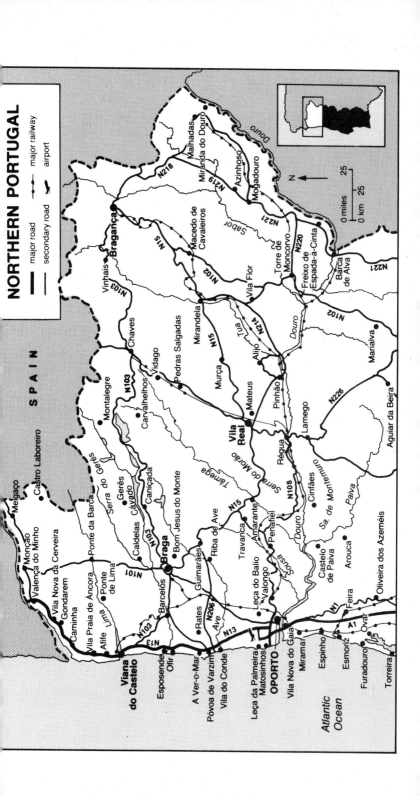

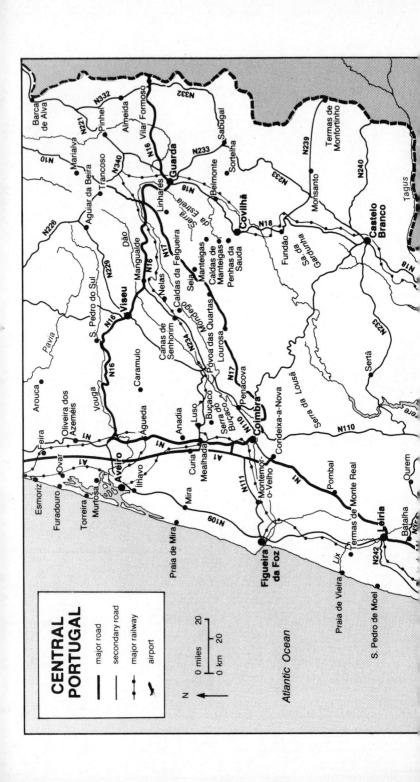

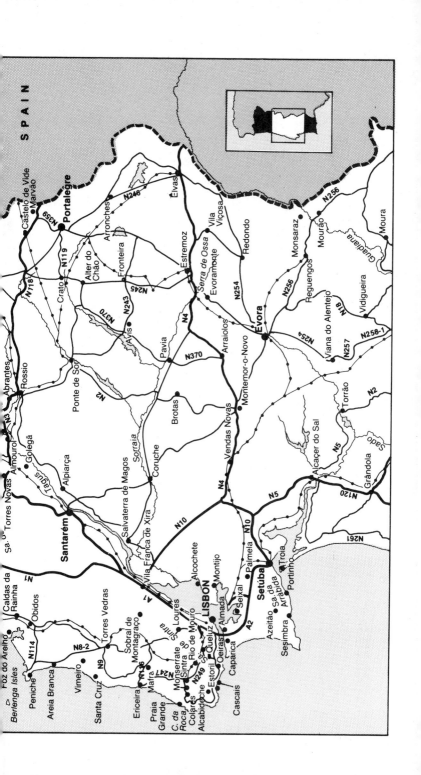

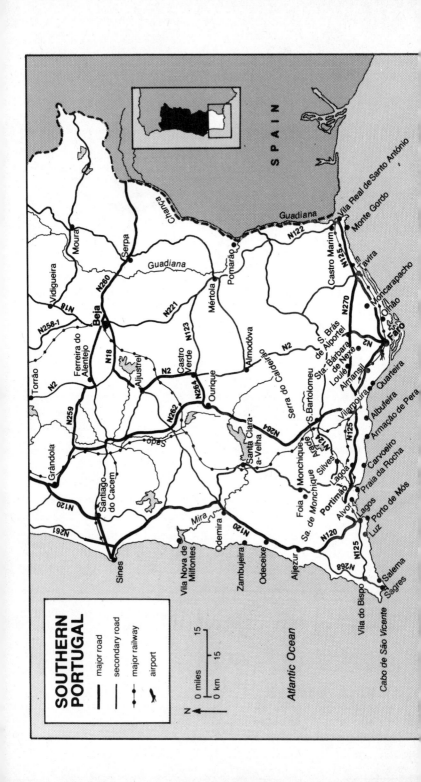

Notes

Fodor's Travel Guides

U.S. Guides

Alaska
Arizona
Atlantic City & the
  New Jersey Shore
Boston
California
Cape Cod
Carolinas & the
  Georgia Coast
The Chesapeake Region
Chicago
Colorado
Disney World & the
  Orlando Area

Florida
Hawaii
Las Vegas
Los Angeles, Orange
  County, Palm Springs
Maui
Miami,
  Fort Lauderdale,
  Palm Beach
Michigan, Wisconsin,
  Minnesota
New England
New Mexico
New Orleans

New Orleans (Pocket
  Guide)
New York City
New York City (Pocket
  Guide)
New York State
Pacific North Coast
Philadelphia
The Rockies
San Diego
San Francisco
San Francisco (Pocket
  Guide)
The South

Texas
USA
Virgin Islands
Virginia
Waikiki
Washington, DC

Foreign Guides

Acapulco
Amsterdam
Australia, New Zealand,
  The South Pacific
Austria
Bahamas
Bahamas (Pocket
  Guide)
Baja & the Pacific
  Coast Resorts
Barbados
Beijing, Guangzhou &
  Shanghai
Belgium &
  Luxembourg
Bermuda
Brazil
Britain (Great Travel
  Values)
Budget Europe
Canada
Canada (Great Travel
  Values)
Canada's Atlantic
  Provinces
Cancun, Cozumel,
  Yucatan Peninsula

Caribbean
Caribbean (Great
  Travel Values)
Central America
Eastern Europe
Egypt
Europe
Europe's Great
  Cities
France
France (Great Travel
  Values)
Germany
Germany (Great Travel
  Values)
Great Britain
Greece
The Himalayan
  Countries
Holland
Hong Kong
Hungary
India,
  including Nepal
Ireland
Israel
Italy

Italy (Great Travel
  Values)
Jamaica
Japan
Japan (Great Travel
  Values)
Kenya, Tanzania,
  the Seychelles
Korea
Lisbon
Loire Valley
London
London (Great
  Travel Values)
London (Pocket Guide)
Madrid & Barcelona
Mexico
Mexico City
Montreal &
  Quebec City
Munich
New Zealand
North Africa
Paris
Paris (Pocket Guide)
People's Republic of
  China

Portugal
Rio de Janeiro
The Riviera (Fun on)
Rome
Saint Martin &
  Sint Maarten
Scandinavia
Scandinavian Cities
Scotland
Singapore
South America
South Pacific
Southeast Asia
Soviet Union
Spain
Spain (Great Travel
  Values)
Sweden
Switzerland
Sydney
Tokyo
Toronto
Turkey
Vienna
Yugoslavia

Special-Interest Guides

Health & Fitness
  Vacations
Royalty Watching

Selected Hotels of
  Europe

Selected Resorts and
  Hotels of the U.S.
Shopping in Europe

Skiing in North America
Sunday in New York